ᴾAUL VIRILIO

Paul Virilio is a challenging and original thinker, whose work on technology, state power and war is increasingly relevant today. Ian James situates Virilio's main texts in their political and historical contexts, as well as providing accessible case studies from contemporary culture and media in order to explain his philosophical concepts.

Taking *Negative Horizon* as a point of departure, Ian James introduces the key themes in Virilio's work, including:

- Speed
- Virtualization
- War
- Politics
- Art

As technological and scientific innovations continue to set the agenda for the present and future development of culture, communications, international economy, military intervention and diverse forms of political organization, Virilio's unique theoretical and critical insights are of enormous value and importance for anyone wishing to understand the nature of modern culture and society.

Ian James is Lecturer in French and Fellow of Downing College at the University of Cambridge. He works in the area of modern French philosophy and literature and his previous publications include *Pierre Klossowski: The Persistence of a Name* (2000) and *The Fragmentary Demand: An Introduction to the Philosophy of Jean-Luc Nancy* (2006).

ROUTLEDGE CRITICAL THINKERS

Series Editor: Robert Eaglestone, Royal Holloway, University of London

Routledge Critical Thinkers is a series of accessible introductions to key figures in contemporary critical thought.

With a unique focus on historical and intellectual contexts, the volumes in this series examine important theorist's:

*   significance
*   motivation
*   key ideas and their sources
*   impact on other thinkers

Concluding with extensively annotated guides to further reading, *Routledge Critical Thinkers* are the student's passport to today's most exciting critical thought.

Already available:

Louis Althusser by Luke Ferretter
Roland Barthes by Graham Allen
Jean Baudrillard by Richard J. Lane
Simone de Beauvoir by Ursula Tidd
Homi K. Bhabha by David Huddart
Maurice Blanchot by Ullrich Haase and William Large
Judith Butler by Sara Salih
Gilles Deleuze by Claire Colebrook
Jacques Derrida by Nicholas Royle
Michel Foucault by Sara Mills
Sigmund Freud by Pamela Thurschwell
Antonio Gramsci by Steve Jones
Stuart Hall by James Procter
Martin Heidegger by Timothy Clark
Fredric Jameson by Adam Roberts

Jean-François Lyotard by Simon Malpas

Jacques Lacan by Sean Homer

Julia Kristeva by Noëlle McAfee

Paul de Man by Martin McQuillan

Friedrich Nietzsche by Lee Spinks

Paul Ricoeur by Karl Simms

Edward Said by Bill Ashcroft and Pal Ahluwalia

Gayatri Chakravorty Spivak by Stephen Morton

Slavoj Žižek by Tony Myers

American Theorists of the Novel: Henry James, Lionel Trilling and Wayne C. Booth by Peter Rawlings

Theorists of the Modernist Novel: James Joyce, Dorothy Richardson & Virginia Woolf by Deborah Parsons

Theorists of Modernist Poetry: T. S. Eliot, T. E. Hulme and Ezra Pound by Rebecca Beasley

Feminist Film Theorists: Laura Mulvey, Kaja Silverman, Teresa de Lauretis and Barbara Creed by Shohini Chaudhuri

Cyberculture Theorists: Manuel Castells and Donna Haraway by David Bell

Theorists of the City: Walter Benjamin, Henri Lefebvre and Michel de Certeau by Jenny Bavidge

For further details on this series, see www.routledge.com/literature/series. asp

PAUL VIRILIO

Ian James

Routledge
Taylor & Francis Group

LONDON AND NEW YORK

First published 2007 by Routledge
2 Park Square, Milton Park, Abingdon, Oxon OX14 4RN

Simultaneously published in the USA and Canada
by Routledge
270 Madison Ave, New York, NY 10016

Routledge is an imprint of the Taylor & Francis Group, an informa business

© 2007 Ian James

Typeset in Perpetua by
Keystroke, 28 High Street, Tettenhall, Wolverhampton
Printed and bound in Great Britain by
TJ International Ltd, Padstow, Cornwall

British Library Cataloguing in Publication Data
A catalogue record for this book is available from the British Library

Library of Congress Cataloging in Publication Data
James, Ian (Ian R.)
Paul Virilio / Ian James. – 1st ed.
     p. cm. – (Routledge critical thinkers)
Includes bibliographical references and index.
1. Virilio, Paul. 2. Culture–Philosophy. 3. Sociology–Philosophy. I. Title.

HM479.V57J36 2007
301.092–dc22   2007003128

ISBN10: 0–415–35963–5   ISBN13: 978–0–415–35963–4 (hbk)
ISBN10: 0–415–35964–3   ISBN13: 978–0–415–35964–1 (pbk)
ISBN10: 0–203–00763–8   ISBN13: 978–0–203–00763–1 (ebk)

In memory of Nick Hanlon

CONTENTS

Series editor's preface   xi
Acknowledgements   xv

WHY VIRILIO?   **1**

KEY IDEAS   **7**

1   The politics of perception   9
2   Speed   29
3   Virtualization   45
4   War   67
5   Politics   89
6   Art   107

AFTER VIRILIO   **121**

FURTHER READING   **127**

Works cited   133
Index   137

SERIES EDITOR'S PREFACE

The books in this series offer introductions to major critical thinkers who have influenced literary studies and the humanities. The *Routledge Critical Thinkers* series provides the books you can turn to first when a new name or concept appears in your studies.

Each book will equip you to approach a key thinker's original texts by explaining her or his key ideas, putting them into context and, perhaps most importantly, showing you why this thinker is considered to be significant. The emphasis is on concise, clearly written guides which do not presuppose specialist knowledge. Although the focus is on particular figures, the series stresses that no critical thinker ever existed in a vacuum but, instead, emerged from a broader intellectual, cultural and social history. Finally, these books will act as a bridge between you and the thinker's original texts: not replacing them but rather complementing what she or he wrote.

These books are necessary for a number of reasons. In his 1997 autobiography, *Not Entitled*, the literary critic Frank Kermode wrote of a time in the 1960s:

> On beautiful summer lawns, young people lay together all night, recovering from their daytime exertions and listening to a troupe of Balinese musicians. Under their blankets or their sleeping bags, they would chat drowsily about the gurus of the time . . . What they repeated was largely hearsay; hence my lunchtime suggestion, quite

impromptu, for a series of short, very cheap books offering authoritative but intelligible introductions to such figures.

There is still a need for 'authoritative and intelligible introductions'. But
this series reflects a different world from the 1960s. New thinkers have
emerged and the reputations of others have risen and fallen, as new research
has developed. New methodologies and challenging ideas have spread
through the arts and humanities. The study of literature is no longer – if it
ever was – simply the study and evaluation of poems, novels and plays. It is
also the study of the ideas, issues and difficulties which arise in any literary
text and in its interpretation. Other arts and humanities subjects have
changed in analogous ways.

With these changes, new problems have emerged. The ideas and issues
behind these radical changes in the humanities are often presented without
reference to wider contexts or as theories which you can simply 'add on' to
the texts you read. Certainly, there's nothing wrong with picking out
selected ideas or using what comes to hand – indeed, some thinkers have
argued that this is, in fact, all we can do. However, it is sometimes forgotten
that each new idea comes from the pattern and development of somebody's
thought and it is important to study the range and context of their ideas.
Against theories 'floating in space', the *Routledge Critical Thinkers* series
places key thinkers and their ideas firmly back in their contexts.

More than this, these books reflect the need to go back to the thinker's
own texts and ideas. Every interpretation of an idea, even the most seemingly innocent one, offers its own 'spin', implicitly or explicitly. To read
only books on a thinker, rather than texts by that thinker, is to deny yourself
a chance of making up your own mind. Sometimes what makes a significant figure's work hard to approach is not so much its style or content as
the feeling of not knowing where to start. The purpose of these books is
to give you a 'way in' by offering an accessible overview of these thinkers'
ideas and works and by guiding your further reading, starting with each
thinker's own texts. To use a metaphor from the philosopher Ludwig
Wittgenstein (1889–1951), these books are ladders, to be thrown away
after you have climbed to the next level. Not only, then, do they equip you
to approach new ideas, but also they empower you, by leading you back to
a theorist's own texts and encouraging you to develop your own informed
opinions.

Finally, these books are necessary because, just as intellectual needs have
changed, education systems around the world – the contexts in which

introductory books are usually read – have changed radically, too. What was suitable for the minority higher education system of the 1960s is not suitable for the larger, wider, more diverse, high-technology education systems of the twenty-first century. These changes call not just for new, up-to-date introductions but new methods of presentation. The presentational aspects of *Routledge Critical Thinkers* have been developed with today's students in mind.

Each book in the series has a similar structure. It begins with an overview of the life and ideas of each thinker and explains why she or he is important. The central section of each book discusses the thinker's key ideas, their context, evolution and reception. Each book concludes with a survey of the thinker's impact, outlining how their ideas have been taken up and developed by others. In addition, there is a detailed final section suggesting and describing books for further reading. This is not a 'tacked-on' section but an integral part of each volume. In the first part of this section you will find brief descriptions of the thinker's key works, then, information on the most useful critical works and, in some cases, on relevant websites. This section will guide you in your reading, enabling you to follow your interests and develop your own projects. Throughout each book, references are given in what is known as the Harvard system (the author and the date of a work cited are given in the text and you can look up the full details in the bibliography at the back). This offers a lot of information in very little space. The books also explain technical terms and use boxes to describe events or ideas in more detail, away from the main emphasis of the discussion. Boxes are also used at times to highlight definitions of terms frequently used or coined by a thinker. In this way, the boxes serve as a kind of glossary, easily identified when flicking through the book.

The thinkers in the series are 'critical' for three reasons. First, they are examined in the light of subjects which involve criticism: principally literary studies or English and cultural studies, but also other disciplines which rely on the criticism of books, ideas, theories and unquestioned assumptions. Second, they are critical because studying their work will provide you with a 'toolkit' for your own informed critical reading and thought, which will make you critical. Third, these thinkers are critical because they are crucially important: they deal with ideas and questions which can overturn conventional understandings of the world, of texts, of everything we take for granted, leaving us with a deeper understanding of what we already knew and with new ideas.

No introduction can tell you everything. However, by offering a way into critical thinking, this series hopes to begin to engage you in an activity which is productive, constructive and potentially life-changing.

Robert Eaglestone

ACKNOWLEDGEMENTS

I would like to offer my warm thanks to all those who have helped with the production of this work, in particular Aileen Storry at Routledge. Special thanks are also due to Robert Eaglestone, who supported the project from the outset and whose careful reading of the manuscript has been greatly appreciated. For the various ways they have helped and supported my work I would like to thank Martin Crowley, Alison Finch, Leslie Hill, Arkady Plotnitsky, and Emma Wilson. I am also very grateful to Downing College Cambridge for the period of research leave which allowed me to complete the book. I would like to thank Ruth Deyermond for all the personal support and all the critical insight she has given throughout the writing of this work. Lastly I would like to dedicate this book to the memory of Nick Hanlon, whose intellectual commitment and warm friendship are greatly missed.

I.J.

WHY VIRILIO?

Paul Virilio is one of the most significant and original thinkers to emerge in the latter half of the twentieth century. His work is fundamentally concerned with questions of perception and embodiment, but also with questions of social and political development. He engages in a sustained manner with a very wide range of issues: with questions of war and military strategy, with the history of cinema, the nature of modern media and telecommunications, and with the state of contemporary cultural and artistic production. The astonishing breadth of his thinking makes him an indispensable point of reference for a wide range of disciplines. His work touches on politics, international relations theory and war studies, on media and social theory, aesthetics, urbanism and environmental thinking. Within this broad range of concerns the question of technology has played a central and determining role. If Virilio is an indispensable contemporary thinker it is perhaps because his work is rooted in a sustained philosophical engagement with the question of technology. Virilio's work shows us how and why technology has been, and will continue to be, fundamental to the shaping of human experience and historical development.

No one would dispute the decisive role played by technological innovation in recent history. The invention of automobile and aerial travel, of telephonic communication, cinema and television had a decisive impact on all aspects human experience from the late nineteenth century onwards. The development of the internet, digital media and mobile phone technology has, more recently, become one of the most visible and all-pervasive indicators of the impact of technological change on social and political life. The great strength of Virilio's work lies in the way it challenges many of our everyday or conventional ways of thinking about technology and the fundamental role it plays in the shaping of our individual and collective experience. We tend to view different technologies in primarily instrumental terms. In other words we tend to see technological devices as tools to be used to certain ends. In so doing we often assume that such tools are, in themselves, neutral or value-free. Yet this view ignores the fact that our everyday activities, our movements, and forms of communication are structured or shaped at a very profound level by the technologies that we use. As the theorist David Kaplan has put it: 'Human life is thoroughly permeated by technology' (Kaplan 2004: xiii). Arguably a technical device or system is never simply or merely a tool, rather: 'Technological devices and systems shape our culture and environment, alter patterns of human activity, and influence who we are and how we live' (Kaplan 2004: xiii). By any account it is difficult to sustain the instrumentalist view of technology as a neutral or value-free tool, since, if tools are made for specific ends or objectives, they are necessarily inserted into a complex web of human life and interaction, or again as Kaplan puts it: 'Humanity and technology are situated in a circular relationship, each shaping and affecting the other' (Kaplan 2004: xv).

Since he began publishing full-length works in 1975 Virilio's writing has directed itself towards a questioning of this circular relation that exists between the human and the technological. He has been most interested in technologies of transmission, that is to say, of transport on the one hand, and of communication on the other. Virilio is perhaps best known as a thinker of speed and of the way in which the increasing speeds of transmission have shaped individual perception, but also social, political and cultural life.

In many ways speed is the key idea which underpins Virilio's writing from the mid 1970s onwards. Yet he is not simply or solely concerned with the acceleration of movement and transmission brought about by modern technology. As will become clear in the opening chapters of this book, for Virilio, speed or relative movement is the element or medium in which our experience unfolds more generally. He is as much interested in slowing down or in deceleration as he is in acceleration. Modern transport and communications technology allows us to move very fast or communicate instantaneously across long distances. Yet it also forces us, as bodies, to spend more time in inert or stationary positions. We remain immobile for long periods of time in plane, train or car seats. We regularly find ourselves equally immobile in front of television or computer screens, or we speak on the telephone to someone we might otherwise visit. If speed is a key idea for Virilio this is perhaps because he is more fundamentally concerned with temporal and spatial organization and the way in which relative movement, that is, both acceleration *and* deceleration, shapes our individual and collective apprehension of time and space.

This concern with temporal and spatial organization has its roots in Virilio's background in architecture and urbanism. He was a professor of architecture at the École Spéciale d'Architecture in Paris between 1969 and 1999, and has generally tended to describe himself as being an urbanist or a thinker of the city. Yet, as has been indicated, this label by no means does justice to the breadth and scope of his engagements. Far from being easily situated within any one discipline Virilio's writing is defined by its ency-clopaedic range of references to many and varied areas of knowledge and by the way in which it makes connections between different areas of human activity (for instance, the development of modern warfare and that of cinema in his seminal work *War and Cinema*, 1989). Yet what makes Virilio's writing so original, and his insights so rich, surprising and sometimes controversial, is the specifically European philosophical and theoretical perspective from which he writes. His discourse on technology, his con-ception of human experience, and of the ways in which we engage with, or understand, the world are deeply influenced by major twentieth-century European thinkers such as Walter Benjamin (1892–1940) and the founding father of phenomenology, Edmund Husserl (1859–1938).

As one critic has noted, Walter Benjamin's theoretical and philosophical writing is informed by the presupposition that 'technology generates new forms' and that 'Technological form precipitates social form' (Leslie 2000: xi). In certain respects Virilio's work can be seen as a continuation of that of Benjamin (who died at the untimely age of forty-eight in 1940). In his famous essay 'The Work of Art in the Age of Mechanical Reproduction' (1936) Benjamin notes:

> During long periods of history, the mode of human sense perception changes with humanity's entire mode of existence. The manner in which human sense perception is organized, the medium in which it is accom-plished, is determined not only by nature but by historical circumstances as well.

> (Benjamin 1974: 216)

For Benjamin, as for Virilio, these historical circumstances which play such a decisive role in the 'organization of perception' (Benjamin 1974: 216) are inextricably bound up with the technological modes which mediate our relationship with the world. In his writing on the nature of modernity Benjamin is interested in analysing 'a sense perception that has been changed by technology' (Benjamin 1974: 235) or as he puts it in an essay on the French poet Charles Baudelaire, he is interested in the way in which 'technology has subjected the human sensorium to a complex kind of training' (Benjamin 1974: 171).

These words written and published by a German thinker in the 1930s could easily have been written by Paul Virilio, a French thinker of Italian origin who was born at the beginning of that decade, in 1932. It is arguably the continuity of Virilio's outlook and approach with some of the most significant and influential thinkers of the early twentieth century that makes his writing so compelling and illuminating as he interrogates the contemporary reality of the late twentieth and early twenty-first centuries. If, however, Virilio follows in Benjamin's footsteps in attempting to understand the 'organization' or the 'training' of sense perception by technological forms, his account of perception itself is indebted to the phenomenological method of thinking founded by Edmund Husserl.

Husserl's philosophical project could (perhaps rather schematically) be best described as the attempt to interrogate the way in which consciousness directs itself towards the objects of perception. It is concerned with the appearance of phenomena in immediate sense perception and seeks to identify the essences or structures which shape the way in which we perceive. In this context Husserl too sought to question the nature of technology and of the modern techno-scientific world view. In his last major work, *The Crisis of European Sciences and Transcendental Phenomenology*, published in 1937, he gave an extended philosophical account of the rise of modern science and of the 'technical thought and activity' it engenders (Husserl 1970: 56). The modern scientific revolution, Husserl argued, has its origin in the mathematics of modern geometry as developed by Galileo in the late sixteenth and early seventeenth centuries. According to this account, Galileo used the new geometry to measure natural phenomena (in particular astronomical events) and in so doing he inaugurated a more general 'mathematization of nature' which came to form the basis of the modern scientific method (Husserl 1970: 23). The methodology of the new mathematics of geometry became, Husserl suggested, dominated by 'calculating technique' (Husserl 1970: 46) and this led to the technization 'of all other methods belonging to natural science' (Husserl 1970: 48). According to Husserl, then, the mathematization of nature ushered in by Galileo's scientific revolution also inaugurated the dominance of a 'technical thinking and activity' (Husserl 1970: 56) within the modern scientific world view. Husserl in no way intended to undermine the truth or universal validity of scientific knowledge. However, he did believe that this 'technization' of thought and activity blinded modern science to its rootedness in everyday sense perception and consciousness of the world. Beneath the abstractions of modern theoretical, mathematical and techno-scientific thinking Husserl sought to rediscover the world of sense perception which constitutes our everyday activities and worldly engagements.

Virilio shares with Husserl the idea that modern experience is shaped by a techno-scientific world view and, like Husserl, he seeks to uncover, rediscover and analyse a more immediate realm of sense perception which precedes the theoretical abstractions of scientific knowledge. Husserl would not, like Virilio and Benjamin, accept that the fundamentals of perception can be shaped or 'trained' by technology, since he aims to demonstrate their universal constancy and logical consistency. Yet his account of the origin of geometry and of modern technical thought and activity is of key importance for Virilio and is referred to at key points in his work (e.g. Virilio 2000d: 71–87, 1993: 101, 118–20, 1991a: 115). Many readers of Virilio will not be, and indeed have not been, familiar with phenomenology as a philosophical movement or tradition. The first chapter of this study will therefore give a more detailed account of what phenomenology as a philosophical theory is. It will also examine the ways in which Virilio's writing is indebted to the phenomenological method and the manner in which he engages with a French tradition of phenomenology which develops Husserl's project in different ways.

This book will show the manner in which Virilio's specific articulation of the phenomenological perspective allows him to develop a highly original and powerful account of the way in which modern technology comes to shape sense perception and the organization of social, political and cultural space. In this respect his thinking is not as divergent from dominant trends within recent French thought as might at first appear. In his important 1992 work *The Possessed Individual* Arthur Kroker argued that 'Contemporary French thought consists of a creative, dynamic and highly original account of technological society' (Kroker 1992: 2). In many ways this is a statement whose implications are still to be fully explored. In this context Virilio is one among a number of prominent French thinkers for whom the question of technology occupies a central position. One need only think, for example, of Foucault's later work, his analyses of 'technologies of power' in works such as *Discipline and Punish* (Foucault 1995) or of 'technologies of the self' (see, for example, Martin 1998). Derrida's discourse on 'originary technics', developed initially in early works such as the 1967 *Of Grammatology* (Derrida 1997) and then more recently in *On Touching* (Derrida 2005) would also be a key point of reference in this context. The term 'technology' is clearly appropriated, transformed or used in very different ways in the work of these different philosophers. Yet in each case such discourses should arguably be seen as complex developments of, or critical responses to, earlier phenomenological accounts of technology (as given by Husserl (see above) or by Martin Heidegger (1889–1976) (see Heidegger 1993: 307–41)).

In the light of this, Virilio emerges as one of a number of highly influential French thinkers who, by inheriting from or moving beyond the tradition of phenomenological thought, continue to provide indispensable conceptual and theoretical resources for the critical understanding of technological modernity and of contemporary social, political and cultural forms. This book will give a detailed introduction to both the philosophical perspectives which inform Virilio's writing, and to the key conceptual innovations which he makes in his theoretical analyses. It will introduce his key arguments relating to the 'becoming virtual' of experience within modern media culture, and will also outline his thinking about war, politics and art. In each chapter careful attention will be paid to the way in which these arguments are consistently rooted in his more fundamental preoccupations with perception, and with the organization of spatial and temporal experience. What follows will not only introduce readers to *what* Virilio thinks and writes about in relation to technological modernity. It will also show *how* he thinks and writes. As will become clear, he writes in a very singular, often disconcerting manner, and advances his arguments in a fragmentary and unsystematic way. Yet, if he writes in this way, he does so for very specific reasons. Virilio's writing is not simply a discourse of 'theory', or one which tries straightforwardly to present his readers with theoretical propositions or truths. Above all, to read Virilio is to be surprised, challenged or provoked. If we are ready to be surprised, and to accept the challenge or provocation of his work, then, Virilio would argue, we may be ready to look at the world in new and different ways.

KEY IDEAS

1

THE POLITICS OF PERCEPTION

Phenomenology, form and the interstices of vision

A preoccupation with the human body lies at the very centre of Virilio's interest in technology. The question of bodily orientation in space and the impact this has on perception and understanding underpins the entirety of his work from the 1960s to the present day. Virilio's response to the development of contemporary technologies and his account of an 'accelerated society' need to be understood within the context of this preoccupation with the body. Throughout his work Virilio aims to affirm the bodily dimension of our experience. He wants to draw our attention to ways in which modern technologies shape the manner in which we experience space and time by orientating our bodies in new and different ways. Above all he wants to draw our attention to the manner in which technologies of speed might diminish the richness and diversity of our situated bodily experience.

Virilio's work has been judged by some to be overly negative or pessimistic with regard to technological development (Virilio 1999: 47) and even, at times, to be somewhat apolitical or conservative (Armitage 2000: 81, 120). Such judgements need to be treated with caution, however. In political terms Virilio's itinerary, like that of many French intellectuals and thinkers of his generation, is broadly of the nonconformist (that is, non-Marxist) left and he has described himself, perhaps disconcertingly, as 'an anarcho-Christian' (Armitage 2001: 20). Yet this Christian commitment is rarely explicitly engaged with as such and Virilio takes pains to put some distance between his personal theological beliefs and the theoretical concerns of his writing. To that extent his approach is very different from other important thinkers of technology such as Jacques Ellul (Ellul 1965). The apparently negative or overly pessimistic tenor of Virilio's works must be understood within the context of the specific discursive strategies, at once provocative and polemical, which inform his writing. Above all his outlook needs to be understood within the context of his explicit philosophical and theoretical commitments. Virilio's primary philosophical engagements are with the phenomenological thought of Edmund Husserl (1859–1938) and of Maurice Merleau-Ponty (1908–61). The insights provided by the early twentieth-century school of psychology known as Gestalt psychology are also of key significance for Virilio. What follows in this first chapter will give an introductory overview of these philosophical and theoretical perspectives and relate them to the way in which bodily experience is affirmed in Virilio's work. It will also relate these theoretical concerns to his background in urbanism and to his early interest in painting.

URBANISM AND *ARCHITECTURE PRINCIPE*

Virilio's commitment to the dimension of situated bodily experience is clearly present in his early work as an urbanist and architect. His background in urbanism dates back to the 1960s and to his collaboration during this period with Claude Parent around the review *Architecture principe*. The general outlook of this review and of those grouped together around it was one of dissidence in relation to the general direction of post-Second World War urban development. This development was perceived to be dominated by an emphasis on the vertical. The perception was that contemporary architecture was far too focused upon the building of structures which would be erected at ever increasing heights. According to the writers of *Architecture principe* the proliferation of skyscrapers and high-rise dwellings was accompanied by a tendency towards a standardization of design whose impact was to disfigure the urban landscape (Joly 2004: 26–7, 57). This standardization of design was, they maintained, characterized by the dominance of construction organized around the 'orthogonal', that is to say, relating to or composed of right angles. Skyscrapers would be built along constructions of horizontal and vertical lines (the outer walls but also the arrangement of windows). A most obvious example of this would, of course, be the World Trade Center in New York which was destroyed in September of 2001.

Against this dominance of the vertical and the orthogonal the collaborators of *Architecture principe* advocated the introduction into contemporary architectural design of what they called 'the oblique function'. Through their championing of 'the oblique function' Virilio and Parent sought to promote a form of urban design and planning which would redefine the relationship maintained between the human body and the surface of the earth. The body would not be located more or less indifferently within an architectural or urban space dominated by excessively tall, right-angled constructions. Rather, the body would be placed within a space organized around inclined surfaces. This environment of inclined surfaces would, as it were, affirm a relation to the movement of the body and its physical situatedness. The 'oblique function', in insisting on a dominance of inclined planes in the design of both ground space and building construction, would demand that a new urban order be thought and a new architectural vocabulary be invented (*Architecture principe*, 1, February 1966, in Virilio and Parent 1996). From the contemporary perspective this revolutionary architectural thinking might appear to be somewhat utopian. Indeed, even at the time Virilio sought to defend his theory against such charges. He argued that the modern attitude to urban space, the physical environment and the consumption of material resources would prove to be unsustainable. Therefore a questioning of the relationship between construction design, spatial planning and the masses of bodies which inhabit cities would, Virilio asserted, be an inevitable and necessary feature of future urbanism (*Architecture principe*, 2, March 1966 in Virilio and Parent 1996).

What is clear is that the 'theory of the oblique' developed by Virilio and Parent favoured an architectural design which would privilege the spatio-temporal first-person experience of the situated human body. If there was a refusal of contemporary development here it was a refusal carried out in the name of a specific affirmation of the spatiality and temporality of bodily experience. Endorsing the work of a contemporary urban designer, Jean-Michel Wilmotte, Virilio recently wrote: 'To neglect this spatial-temporal sphere would imply a total misreading of the world's future metropolisation, would strip all objects and signs of their very meaning' (Wilmotte 1999: 10). This comment is entirely consistent with Virilio's early work of the 1960s. The gesture of refusal in relation to dominant contemporary trends which characterized the review *Architecture principe* was not a form of conservatism nor pessimistic nostalgia for a past urban space. Rather it was an attempt to address a fundamental orientation of bodily experience. It aimed to uncover and promote a different or dissident understanding of architectural design. This was based on the hope that future and hitherto unthought possibilities of development might be conceived. This twofold gesture of refusal and affirmation can be found in Virilio's work as a whole. He refuses certain aspects of contemporary development but does so only to affirm the possibilities of the human body and the diverse ways it can be situated within space. This twofold gesture of refusal and affirmation can be understood more clearly when related to Virilio's commitment to the philosophical perspective of phenomenology (see box, pp. 13–14).

PHENOMENOLOGY

The reference to phenomenology in Virilio's work offers the key to understanding the central place occupied by the body and the relation of technology to bodily experience. Allusions to phenomenological thought occur throughout his work, most prominently in references to Husserl in *The Insecurity of Territory* (Virilio 1993: 118), in *Polar Inertia* (Virilio 2000d: 71–87) and in *The Lost Dimension* (Virilio 1991a: 115). The phenomeno-logical perspective is also present in his persistent appeal to aspects of Merleau-Ponty's thinking, in for example *The Vision Machine* (Virilio 1994b: 7), and *The Art of the Motor* (Virilio 1995: 81, 141). What interests Virilio in the work of both philosophers is the idea that 'space is limited to the world of sensible experience and beyond that there is no longer any space worthy of the name' (Virilio 1995: 141). From the perspective of phenomenology space is not simply the extension of three dimensions such as it can measured by mathematics. Phenomenology is not interested in traditional debates relating to the question of whether space is a substantive thing in itself or simply a relation between things (theories known as sub-stantivalism and relationalism respectively). Rather phenomenology thinks space as that which is first and foremost *experienced*. It thinks of space as spatiality, that is to say, as a spatial perception or awareness which is insep-arable from the manner in which our bodies are positioned. Spatiality is inseparable from our capacity to sense, touch and see within the context of a specific bodily orientation. It is only on the basis of this prior experience of spatiality, the argument runs, that we can come to some abstract or theoretical understanding of space. The theoretical understanding of space as the extension of three dimensions (or indeed any other theoretical or scientific understanding of space) would not be possible if we did not first encounter space as situated and lived spatiality.

This argument is given most clearly and fully by Husserl in his lectures of 1907 on *Thing and Space* (Husserl 1997) and is developed in different ways within the phenomenological tradition after Husserl. It is developed, for instance, in the account of existential spatiality given by Martin Heidegger in *Being and Time* (Heidegger 1962: 135–48) or in the account given by Merleau-Ponty of space and perception in *Phenomenology of Perception* (Merleau-Ponty 2002: 116 ff.). What is important to note here is that, for the phenomenologist, our experience or perception of space is inseparable from the positioning and movement of the body in relation to its surroundings. Our gaze on to the world can be thought of only as a gaze which is first and foremost embodied. Our experience of the world might, for instance, be very different if we were not upright animals and did not have eyes placed at the front of our head. Can one imagine, for instance, how the world might look if we had one eye positioned on either side of our heads and could see forwards and backwards simultaneously?

PHENOMENOLOGY

Phenomenology is a philosophical project which aims to describe the character of consciousness in the most clear and systematic way. Its concern, therefore, is with what appears (i.e. with *phenomena*) in lived sensible experience. The existence of phenomena independent of experience is not posed here, nor is it thought to be a viable philosophical question. The founding father of phenomenology, Edmund Husserl (1859–1938), sought to interrogate phenomena in terms of the way in which we direct our consciousness to them. What is important to the phenomenologist is the manner in which objects appear to consciousness according to the intentions we have towards them. The phenomenologist interrogates those intentional structures or abstract elements which shape the directedness of our consciousness. It is on the basis of these structures of directedness or intentionality that the world of sensible appearances is constituted for us as meaningful and intelligible. The aim of Husserlian phenomenological investigation was to isolate the meaning-constituting structures which make consciousness possible. Husserl rejected the claims of empiricism. According to the philosophy of empiricism the logical laws of sense and meaning can be located in actual mental activity, in, for instance, the physiology of brain function. To this extent Husserl's philosophy is concerned not with physiological or neurological properties but with the logical conditions of possibility of experience. It excludes or brackets off any specific or particular content of experience. These logical conditions are, for Husserl, both universal and necessary. To this extent his philosophy can be placed within the tradition of idealism such as it developed in the wake of the eighteenth-century German philosopher Emmanuel Kant. Husserl affirmed the existence of what he termed the transcendental ego. With the term 'transcendental ego' he aimed to describe an impersonal realm distinct from the empirical self or subjective ego. The transcendental ego, for Husserl, works to constitute the world for us by way of meaning-constituting structures and abstract logical elements. Husserl maintained that all knowledge, all theoretical, rational or scientific endeavour depend upon and are derived from acts of consciousness and the intentional structures which give them life. The logical priority given to immediate consciousness or perception over theoretical abstraction or speculative reason is continued in the phenomenological tradition after Husserl, in, for instance, the different forms of existential phenomenology developed by Martin Heidegger, Maurice Merleau-Ponty and Jean-Paul Sartre. In their different ways each of these three thinkers criticizes Husserl's emphasis on ideality and abstraction; they question the existence of the transcendental ego and affirm the impossibility of isolating formal logical structures within conscious acts. As existential phenomenologists they shift the emphasis away from ideal or logical essences in favour of structures of 'being-in-the-world'. By this account the intentional acts through which meaning-constitution occurs are possible because of our prior insertion into a series of pragmatic worldly engagements which both precede and exceed the possibility of their isolation as abstract forms. Merleau-Ponty, for example, replaces the transcendental ego with the idea of the body-subject. Neither mind nor body in the traditional sense, Merleau-Ponty's body-subject experiences the world as meaningful only in so far as it is orientated in space and inserted into more or less diffuse horizons of sense and purpose. These horizons exist prior to conscious intentionality or will and constitute the 'intentional arc' of the body-subject, that is, the field of purposeful engagements on the basis of which meaningful experience can occur. The existential phenomenology of Merleau-Ponty maintains Husserl's key insistence that all abstract or theoretical knowledge must be viewed as secondary to and derived from the life of immediate consciousness, perception and experience.

This question of the embodied or situated gaze is fundamental to the way in which Virilio understands our relationship to the world. Our gaze shapes our encounter with worldly space as it is immediately experienced in embodied perception. He speaks, for instance, of: 'the real horizon of the world, towards which, Merleau-Ponty tells us, *we first move by way of our gaze* [*le regard*]' (Virilio 1995: 81). For Virilio it is above all the 'mobility and motility of the body' which allow our perceptions of the world to occur and with this an experience of ourselves as worldly spatial creatures (Virilio 1993: 260). He is interested in how the landscape of places and things will look or appear differently depending on the way in which they are approached. As an example of this he cites the situation of a passenger on a train viewing the passing scenery: 'it is the movements of my body that are producing this landscape . . . a bit like a passenger on a train sees trees and horses darting past, sees hills bending away' (Virilio 2005a: 30). When travelling by train or car we often think of ourselves simply as passing through space. Yet from the phenomenological perspective this everyday interpretation of our experience is possible only because we first experience the figures and forms surrounding us in a rather different manner: the tree which we might otherwise approach on foot, see looming above us and then touch or even climb, emerges rapidly into our field of vision, reduced in size, and sweeps past, untouched and unclimbed and has disappeared in an instant. The spread of the landscape which might otherwise surround and envelop us is deformed by rapid movement; it is not something experienced in its material dimensions as such since our body does not experience the fatigue or the extended delay of passing across it on foot. In each case (travelling by train or on foot) the world appears to us or is perceived in a very different manner. This example demonstrates the central importance of bodily perception in Virilio's thinking. It indicates, clearly, why the reality of movement and speed remains so fundamental. Movement and speed are not, for Virilio, simply thematic concerns. Rather they are structuring principles of the manner in which we experience the space of the world. In this respect Virilio's, primarily phenomenological, understanding of space is different from that of science. He does not, as it were, think in three dimensions, but holds rather that the 'dimensions of space are only fleeting apparitions, in the same way that things are visible only in the trajectory of the gaze, this gaze that is the eye and that defines place' (Virilio 2005a: 118).

What this phenomenological perspective suggests is that Virilio's approach to the world, and to the way the world is experienced, is removed from our everyday understanding. Husserl describes this everyday understanding as the 'natural attitude'. According to the natural attitude we assume more or less unreflectively that we live in a world of things which are exterior to us and exist objectively in an extended space and in a linear time. We assume that there is a distinct separation between these things and our consciousness of them, or our subjective engagements with them. The phenomenological perspective does not, of course, deny the objective existence of things. It does, however, insist that this objective existence can be understood only relative to, and on the basis of, our shared perceptions of these things within a lived (that is, embodied) spatial and temporal experience. We always encounter or perceive objects within the context of the shared forms of sense or meaning that are bestowed upon them. Things appear to us as meaningful entities only in the context of such a shared horizon of sense.

Virilio explicitly affirms this understanding of the existence of things at the beginning of *Negative Horizon*: 'forms, things, emit and receive, they emit a sensible reality and what they have undergone, they receive and return the totality of the sense of their milieu and their immediate surroundings' (Virilio 2005a: 27). So if I walk into a room, see a desk, sit at it and begin to write, I do so because the desk appears to me as an object which is intelligible and meaningful for me only against the background of a prior horizon of sense. This horizon of sense or meaning determines the context of the room, the functional nature of the space within the room and therefore the purpose or sense-value that the objects placed in there will have for me. According to the natural attitude of everyday understanding all these things – that is, the study, the space within, the desk and writing materials – are entities whose identity is simply given in the presence of the object itself. Everyday understanding tells me that I encounter these things as objects of my will and decision. It allows me to assume that the identity or sense value of such objects exists independently of my encounter with them and of the decisions I might make with respect to them. A central premise of the phenomenological approach is that the unreflective natural attitude which presupposes this straightforward objectivity or givenness of things conceals or obscures the manner in which objects in the world actually appear to us. They are not simply 'there', rather they are encountered as meaningful in the spatial and temporal orientation of an embodied perception and within the context of shared horizons of sense. The aim of the phenomenological approach, then, is to suspend the natural attitude and with that our everyday understanding of the world and to interrogate that layer of more primordial experience which lies concealed beneath it. It allows an inquiry into the way in which things appear to us in the first instance and into the more original horizon of sense-giving which makes that appearance intelligible as such. Virilio's phenomenological outlook is perhaps the most difficult initial aspect of his work to understand or assimilate. This is perhaps because we tend to be firmly wedded to the natural attitude described by Husserl. Perhaps more easy to understand or assimilate is the extended account of his early experience as a painter which Virilio gives at the beginning of *Negative Horizon*. This personal account of his early experiments with painting more clearly exemplifies what is at stake in his commitment to phenomenology and to the phenomenological questioning of perception and embodiment.

PAINTING

The rejection of abstract formalism which characterizes Virilio's relation to architecture and urbanism also underpins his interest in painting. In so far as this interest in painting also exemplifies his phenomenological outlook, it can shed light on the method or approach of his writing as a whole. In his foreword to the 1984 work *Negative Horizon* Virilio comments at length about his motivations as a painter and the impact of painting on his approach to the world.

Negative Horizon is arguably one of Virilio's most important works. It gathers together and gives a unified exploration of the key concerns which run throughout his writing. It engages at length the question of speed and with the science of 'dromology' (this will be dealt with further in Chapter 3). It investigates the impact of accelerated speeds of transmission on perception, on the experience of global space, and on military, social and political organization. All these concerns will be explored more fully in the following chapters. To this extent his extended meditation on painting in the foreword to *Negative Horizon* almost demands to be read as a conscious reflection upon the general theoretical and methodological approach of his writing. From his earliest days, Virilio asserts, he was 'resistant to the formulas of mathematics but open to the figures of geometry and geography' (Virilio 2005a: 26). As a painter, and in particular as a painter of still life, he is interested, not in mathematical abstraction, but rather in shapes, figures and forms. Virilio expresses this in the following terms: 'Figures always spoke to me . . . I found shapes all around me expressive' (Virilio 2005a: 26). As young boy he could remember and trace on the blackboard the contours of maps and varied geographical forms but the language of dates, arithmetic and formulae was, conversely, entirely foreign to him. His interest as a painter, therefore, is with the appearance of forms rather than with the representation of objects as such. He is interested in the way figures and forms appear in perception prior to their identification as this or that (mathematically) measurable object. Put another way, he is interested in visible forms prior to their designation in language as this or that identifiable thing:

> it was already clear to me that we could turn our inquiry into the silent appearance of objects, of things, of figures, and that this inquiry would necessarily become an art of painting the pictorial as questioning and not as representation.
>
> (Virilio 2005a: 27)

It may be recalled once more that Virilio's interest in architecture was defined by a preoccupation with a fundamental experience of bodily situatedness and a rejection of abstract formalism. In the same way his interest in painting is defined by a concern with the immediate perception of forms and with a rejection of those categories (mathematical or linguistic) through which they might more conventionally be represented. The aim of his painting, he asserts, was: 'To reflect . . . the phenomenology of figures, the origin of geometry', since 'There is no abstraction, everything presents a figure' (Virilio 2005a: 27).

This is the meaning that Virilio explicitly gives to his painterly activity and which can be extended to his work as a whole. His endeavour is not simply an attempt to represent the forms of the sensible world around him. He aims rather to uncover that which is hidden from our everyday view, to interrogate the more fundamental relation of the perceiving body to its surroundings, to discover 'the richness, the affluence of that which does not appear, the life of that which seems to be absent' (Virilio 2005a: 28).

FORMS

If Virilio's account of painting draws our attention to the more general role played by phenomenology in his work it also highlights the importance of another theoretical perspective underpinning his writing, namely the psychology of forms or what is also known as 'Gestalt psychology' (see box, pp. 19–21). As has been indicated, painting, for Virilio, should not be seen simply as representation but rather as a questioning of the 'silent appearance' 'of objects, of things, of figures'. In both phenomenology and Gestalt psychology the question of the appearance of forms is of central importance. Virilio's interest in the psychology of form is centred principally around the relation that forms or figures maintain with the 'perceptual whole' to which they belong. His argument is that, in our everyday engagements and perceptual habits, we recognize certain things very easily but pass over, ignore or fail to see other aspects of the world around us. This is because certain forms, and the relation they have to their surroundings or background of appearance, are deeply familiar to us and provide the structuring principles with which we organize our habitual perception of the world. Once again Virilio refers to the figures of geometry: 'While we perceive circles, spheres, cubes or corners perfectly, our perception of intervals, of the interstices between things, between people is far less acute' (Virilio 2005a: 29). In fact Virilio's preoccupation is far more centred on that which escapes, or is obscured by, the forms and figures with which we are most familiar. Our 'perception of intervals' or of 'the interstices between things' is so much less acute because, in our habituation to received figures, we structure our general view of the world according to a principle of sameness. Perceiving according to this principle of sameness, we systematically exclude the 'in-between' or that which does not show itself clearly in the relation of a familiar form to its background. This, for Virilio, is not a neutral tendency but has ethical and political implications:

> We pass our time and our lives in contemplating what we have already contemplated, and by this we are most insidiously imprisoned. This redundancy constructs our habitat, we construct by analogy and by resemblance, it is our architecture. Those who perceive, or build differently, or elsewhere, are our hereditary enemies.
>
> (Virilio 2005a: 37)

It is clear from this citation that Virilio sees our tendency to structure our perception of the world around resemblances and similarities in negative terms. In succumbing to such a tendency we not only risk a kind of perceptual incarceration, that is, an inability to engage with the diverse and unfamiliar, but we also lay the grounds for hostility or even violence towards those who see differently.

GESTALT PSYCHOLOGY

Gestalt psychology developed in Germany in the early twentieth century in response to trends dominant within the general discipline of psychology in the late nineteenth century. Nineteenth-century psychology tended to endorse the theory of associationism, that is, the doctrine that the content of consciousness could be explained by the association and reassociation of initially disparate sensory elements. Associationism was, then, essentially atomistic in nature: the immediate given of sensory elements could be combined only through their contiguity in actual experience, that is, their positioning and contact alongside each other, and through the reinforcement of these contacts by repeated association over time. Associationism was, then, an essentially empiricist theory which privileged the content of experience over pre-given structures of the mind. Influenced by the phenomenological philosophy of Edmund Husserl, Gestalt psychologists, such as Wolfgang Köhler (1887–1967), Max Wertheimer (1880–1943) and Kurt Koffka (1886–1941), challenged associationism, arguing for the existence of objects and relational forms which would be different from collections of sensations. They rejected the notion that sensory elements are the building blocks of mental life and maintained that it is the existence of dynamic structures which determine the appearance of forms and what we perceive, within them, as foreground or background, part or whole. The ground of mental life was not to be seen in atomistic terms, but rather as the experience of forms, that is, organic unities or wholes which manifest themselves within the spatial and temporal field of perception or representation. Fundamental to this perspective is the notion that any sensible object which presents itself in perception does so only in relation to a background. This is true not just for visible objects but for any sensory experience (for instance, a sound is identified against the background of silence or of other sounds from which it detaches itself). Objects or sensations are never experienced in isolation but always within a determining relation of a figure to its background. This means that, in everyday perception, the way in which we habitually organize the relation of figure to background plays a decisive role. Nothing would be coherent to us at all if our perceptual field was not structured in a hierarchy of different plans, in which certain figures occupied a more prominent and visible place in relation to their background, and others were not marginalized or given a less visible position. This means that perception and the different perspectives which organize perception are a function of both organizational unities *and* those habitual processes of viewing which relate those unities to each other hierarchically. Whilst interested in the subjective field of perception the Gestalt psychologists nevertheless worked as scientists and were committed to testing their insights and developing their theories in a manner consistent with the techniques of experimental science. In stressing the primacy of perceptual wholes over the atomism of sensation they sought, however, to take the science of psychology beyond the reductionism which seeks to return all mental life to the physiology of brain function.

This concern with received habits of seeing and with the 'imprisonment' of perception within the familiar means that Virilio is not just interested in form but also with its opposite, 'antiform'. Painting is described by Virilio not just as an attempt to 'reflect the phenomenology of figures' but also as a 'hunt for figures of intervals' (Virilio 2005a: 30) and as a desire to 'flush out the antiform' (Virilio 2005a: 31). He says of his project as a painter: 'I was convinced that there are certain species of [antiform], unknown, unperceived, families, races, and I was quite determined to discover them and make an inventory of them' (Virilio 2005a: 31). The interest in the psychology of form parallels the interest in phenomenology in so far as the aim is once again to move beyond those everyday appearances which shape our normal understanding. For Virilio, both these theoretical perspectives suspend the 'natural attitude' identified by Husserl and allow him to uncover richer and more diverse possibilities of seeing, to look at the world from a different angle.

By way of example one might cite here those silhouette or line drawings which, depending on the manner in which they are viewed, allow for the perception of a different image. One of the most famous of these is the old lady/young lady optical illusion, a picture which, when initially viewed, appears to be an image of an aging woman (Fig. 1). With a slight effort, placing a different emphasis on the relation of the black areas of the image to its white background, the figure of a young woman emerges to take the place of the previous image. At that point the viewer of the image, depending on the way the different forms are viewed in different relations of foreground and background, can, at will, see alternately a younger or older woman.

Another example would be the classic image, drawn from the canon of Gestalt psychology, which shows what might initially appear to be a white vase or goblet against a black background (Fig. 2). For the vase to appear we must assume white as the foreground. If, however, we take the black areas as the foreground then the image becomes one of two facial profiles placed opposite each other. Again, with an effort one can make one or the

Figure 1

Figure 2

other image emerge. If one approaches the image with a more or less indifferent assumption in relation to foreground and background it is likely that an oscillation between vase/goblet and opposing faces will be perceived. In each case the form is visible or intelligible as such only in relation to a perception of the whole of the image. The visible image takes on a specific form on the basis of an assumption we make about the structuring of that whole. What is true for such visual puzzles or optical illusions is true for the forms around us in the world. With a sustained effort, Virilio maintains, the world around us can offer up all kinds of possibilities of perception, although the 'antiforms' we might encounter will perhaps emerge only fleetingly: 'the vision of the between-world was extremely fragile . . . the antiform only persisted as long as this effort was kept up, afterwards form reclaimed its stake' (Virilio 2005a: 31). What is important for Virilio is the way in which his career as a painter trained him in this art of sustained effort, an art of seeing between forms or of viewing in such a way that what might normally be hidden is suddenly brought into the light of day. The art of painting has as its goal 'to render the invisible visible' (Virilio 2005a: 33).

THE INTERSTICES OF VISION

As has been suggested the aim of this interrogation of antiforms, of the in-between or the invisible, is not purely aesthetic but also has an ethical and a political dimension. Our preoccupation with habitual forms and ways of seeing is arguably related to a whole cultural politics which favours same-ness over difference. Virilio puts this in the following terms: 'The eclipse of antiforms appeared to me to be the consequence of a sort of imperial-ism of apprehension. Vision, my vision, was rejecting, in the same way as Western culture, the ground, margins, difference' (Virilio 2005a: 32). This politicizing of perception may seem surprising. We find it easy to accept that all kinds of broader understanding of social reality are political (for example, the way we view those from other cultures or classes). That the very basics of the way in which we perceive the world of appearances may be political is perhaps less easy to admit. In this context Virilio talks of the manner in which perspective is always constructed on the basis of a hierarchy: 'Perspective is only a hierarchy of perception and there are probably as many perspectives as there are visions of the world, of cultures, of ways of life' (Virilio 2005a: 35). In relation to seeing or viewing we tend to think of perspective as the appearance of an object in depth. Alternatively we think of it as the technique of representing three-dimensional objects and depth relations on a two-dimensional surface (as in, for instance, Renaissance painting). This, of course, implies a conception of space as mathematically measurable extension, that is, the abstract or theoretical understanding which Virilio's phenomenological approach avoids (in favour of the lived spatiality of bodily perception). One should not, therefore, confuse Virilio's statements on the politics and hierarchy of perspective with any scientific or quasi-scientific proposition. He is not suggesting that the multiple and culture-bound perspectives he invokes are *scientifically* of equal value to the notion of perspective conceived as a (geometrically measurable) repre-sentation of objects in depth. He may well be suggesting, however, that the decision our culture makes to privilege the universally valid, geometrical notion of perspective over the rich and diverse perspectives of embodied perception is a culturally value-laden and politically charged fact. Either way, our perspectival habits are not neutral or value-free.

Virilio's comments about painting at the beginning of *Negative Horizon*, informed as they are by the theoretical concerns and insights of both phenomenology and Gestalt psychology, suggest quite clearly that his overall approach to the world should not be confused or conflated with any straightforward representation of social reality. Nor should they be confused with conventional political or sociological analysis. Rather his writing orientates itself primarily around the question of vision and seeing. This, as has been shown, is inseparable from the question of the body's situatedness, and from the way it moves through space. It is inseparable also from the codes, forms or habits which structure everyday perception. Claude Parent, Virilio's collaborator on the review *Architecture principe*, describes the man and his work in the following terms:

> Paul Virilio is a reader of reality. A Master of reading the real, he is not an analyst in this area but rather a creator. In the present he tracks down the future. He sorts, he chooses, he gathers together; in his hands the most minute indicators are pieces of evidence which overturn the hierarchy of the present; he is an archaeologist of the future.
>
> (*Architecture Principe*, 6, September–October 1966, in Virilio and Parent 1996)

Virilio, as a 'reader of the real', does not simply describe or analyse reality, conceived, as it were, as an objective given of shared spaces, things, events. His interest in embodied perception and antiforms leads him to question received ways of seeing and understanding in order 'positively to reinvent our vision of the world' so that we may then 'change our view' and 'change our lives' (Virilio 2005a: 38). As will become clear in the ensuing chapters, Virilio's account of technological development and of contemporary war, politics and culture may at times seem rather negative. Yet it is important to understand this apparent negativity of his writing within the context of the conceptual and perceptual strategies outlined here. Virilio is convinced that 'everything that will determine the novelty, the originality of tomorrow, is already present in the moment, concealed in the everyday vision of each person' (Virilio 2005a: 29). In his interrogation of the 'interstices of vision' and in his questioning of the politics of perception and received ways of viewing, he is aiming to uncover ignored or hidden realities within our contemporary experience. His assumption is that the hidden or obscured realities of today may well define our collective future experience. Most importantly, Virilio does not do this in order to mourn some kind of pre-technological past era. His questioning is intended to be enabling, to allow us to proceed and think differently with respect to the dominant technological tendency of our time.

Above all, Virilio's endeavour aims at the retrieval of those hidden layers of bodily experience and perception which he describes in relation to his work as a painter and which he affirmed in his thinking as an urbanist. He wishes to 'rediscover touch, the touch of walking . . . all the signs of another divergence, of a return to the physical, to matter, the signs of a rematerialisation of the body and of the world' (Virilio 1999: 49). This is an endeavour which, like painting, is artistic as much as it is critical, and, as Claude Parent noted, is more creative than it is strictly analytical. Virilio has described himself as an 'art critic of technology' (Armitage 2001: 25). Any approach to his texts which reads them simply as a series of empirical or theoretical propositions about modern technology, war and society is likely to gravely misconstrue the nature of the insights afforded and to badly misunderstand their discursive and rhetorical force. Virilio's writing tells us first and foremost that we need to consider carefully the way we view the world, that we need to question our received ways of seeing and attend closely to bodily experience. This is a writing which seeks to uncover 'our silent life', to reveal that which may lie hidden behind the conventional forms and images of the sensible world. It is a writing that demands a different encounter with reality in the name of new and different ways of coding and recoding shared perceptions of the world.

SUMMARY

Virilio's key preoccupation is with the relation of technology to bodily situatedness. He is interested in the way perception is structured through the orientation of the body within its physical and technological environment. This preoccupation is evident in his early work as an architect and urbanist but also in his career as a painter. His comments on his early career as a painter highlight the key philosophical and theoretical perspectives which underpin his writing as a whole, namely those of phenomenology and Gestalt psychology. Both these perspectives lead Virilio to refuse habitual ways of seeing or understanding the world in order to interrogate layers of perception and experience which may be hidden from view. Conventional ways of seeing and understanding can be viewed as value-laden and inhibit our ability to engage with the richness and diversity of perceptual life. The apparent pessimism of Virilio's approach to technology and its impact on social and political change needs to be understood within the context of this affirmation of bodily experience. Virilio's writing should be viewed in the light of his commitment to a politics of perception which aims to uncover possible futures concealed within the present. It allows us to respond critically or divergently to the goals which technologies and technological thinking propose for themselves.

2

SPEED

Dromology, speed-space
and light-time

Virilio is perhaps most widely known as a thinker of speed and as a practitioner of the 'science of speed', that is, 'dromology'. Dromology and other terms such as 'dromoscopy' and 'dromosphere' are neologisms coined by Virilio himself and derive from the Greek *dromos*, meaning race or racecourse. The term 'science' here should not, of course, be confused with natural or physical science but should be taken in the sense of science as a body of knowledge, discipline or methodological activity. Dromology, then, is that body of knowledge concerned specifically with the phenomenon of speed, or more precisely, with the way speed determines or limits the manner in which phenomena appear to us. According to Virilio we cannot properly approach the reality of social, political or military history unless we first realize that social space, political space and military space are, at a decisive and fundamental level, shaped by vectors of movement and the speed of transmission with which these vectors of movement are accomplished.

The emphasis placed on movement and on speed of transmission as key forces which shape social and political space leads Virilio to make sometimes startling claims. In *Speed and Politics*, for instance, he asserts the following: 'there was no industrial revolution', but only a 'dromocratic revolution; there is no democracy, only dromocracy' (Virilio 1986: 46). He has insisted in works such as *Negative Horizon* that 'movement governs the event' and that the ever increasing speeds which have determined movement in modern society have 'caused the traditional political structures to implode' (Virilio 2005a: 105, 60). However startling or peremptory such assertions may at first appear they are made within the context of a more general argument which is developed in a fairly systematic fashion across the range of Virilio's writing from the 1970s to the present day. In an interview with the media theorist Friedrich Kittler he summarizes his view that contemporary global society has hit a 'wall of acceleration' (Armitage 2001: 97–8). The argument runs as follows: societies have hitherto developed according to a logic of ever increasing acceleration of the speed of both transport and communication; we have moved from the age of horseback or horse-drawn locomotion to that of the railway, from the age of the telephone to that of radio transmission and then to television and digital or information technology. The 'progress' of each age in relation to that preceding it has implicitly been defined by the accelerated transmission afforded by new technological means: train travel exceeds that of horse-drawn locomotion, the aeroplane that of the train, the digital transmission of data outstrips the speeds of transmission accomplished by the technologies that came before. Virilio's contention is that contemporary society is reaching a critical point at which further acceleration may soon no longer be possible. If, in the age of the internet or digital and satellite communication, information can be transmitted quasi-instantaneously worldwide, or if, as planners and aviation engineers expect, hypersonic aeroplanes will soon be able to traverse the globe in around two hours, will society not reach a point where any future progress of acceleration is impossible? What are the broader implications for a society which has reached such a stage? This, at least, is the state of affairs Virilio is referring to, and the question he is posing when he talks about our society standing at a limit or at the 'wall' of acceleration.

Speed, then, is the element which unifies all of Virilio's writing about the impact of modern technologies on perception and on social, political and military development. It is, for Virilio, both the medium in which collective experience unfolds and a key motor or driving force which underpins the historical dynamic of that experience. Speed, as he puts it in characteristically hyperbolic terms, is 'a *destiny* at the same time as being a *destination*' (Virilio 2005a: 42). The following chapters will explore in more detail the scope of Virilio's 'dromological' thinking in relation to his specific critical concerns (the becoming virtual of experience, war, politics and art respectively). However, it is worth stressing at this point that speed is not just a more or less omnipresent and determining factor across the body of Virilio's thinking and writing. It is also a crucial factor in shaping the way he thinks and writes. This chapter will explore further the fundamental status of speed within Virilio's theoretical perspective but will highlight also the manner in which dromological thinking and writing are themselves governed by a rhetoric or discursive style which arises directly from the experience of speed and its impact on perception.

SPEED-SPACE AND THE DROMOSPHERE

As was indicated in the preceding chapter the fundamental role accorded to speed in Virilio's writing is rooted in his phenomenological approach and in the emphasis phenomenological thought places upon the location and orientation of the body within its physical environment. The world of things appears to us in the first instance as a world of immediate perception. This means that the apprehension of objects in our field of vision results from the various movements these objects undergo relative to those of the body. Space in this context is not, it may be recalled, the geometrical or extended space of three dimensions. Rather it is viewed in terms of what might be called a prior 'spatiality' strictly limited to the world of sensible appearance. For Virilio this phenomenological space is, therefore, above all a space defined by relative movements and by the relative or changing speed of those movements, that is, by forces of acceleration and deceleration. In the 1984 work *Lost Dimension* he puts this in the following terms: 'acceleration and deceleration . . . are the only dimensions of space, of a *speed-space*, a dromospheric space which would no longer be defined as *substantial and extensive*, as volume, mass, density . . . extension or surface' (Virilio 1991a: 102). This is explicitly not the space proper to geometry or to, say, Newtonian physics. Rather the existence of speed-space and of the dromosphere needs to be understood *in purely phenomenological terms* in the light of two determining factors: first, the movement of things or perceived objects in relation to that of the body and second, the light (solar, electric etc.) which illuminates those objects for perception and therefore acts as the condition of possibility of vision as such.

On a number of different occasions Virilio has insisted that speed is not itself a phenomenon but rather a relation between phenomena (e.g. Virilio 1994b: 74, 1999: 14, 2000d: 45). He has even gone further than this, suggesting that speed is an environment or a milieu (Virilio 1999: 14). Speed may normally be taken rather straightforwardly as the relative rate of movement of an object through space, the measure of that rate, or as simple rapidity of motion. As always with Virilio's thinking we need to push at the limits of our usual way of viewing or understanding the key terms with which he works in order to grasp the meaning they have for him. In *Open Sky* he takes pains to differentiate his understanding of speed from its everyday meaning: 'In effect, speed does not solely permit us to move more easily, above all it permits us to see, to hear, to perceive and thus to conceive more intensively the present world' (Virilio 1997a: 12). In this sense speed is both enabling in so far as it permits us to see, but also limiting in so far as it determines the manner in which things appear to us, or as Virilio puts it in *Polar Inertia*, 'the truth of phenomena is always limited by the speed of their sudden appearance [*surgissement*]' (Virilio 2000d: 82).

In order to understand what is at stake here the example of rapid travel by train or car may once again be of help. We saw in the last chapter that Virilio himself alluded to the experience of the train traveller looking out on to the landscape. In the chapter entitled 'Dromoscopy' in *Negative Horizon* this analysis of vision and movement is developed in a much more extended manner, referring to the perceptions of the car traveller as he or she looks through the windscreen of a vehicle in motion. Virilio's description is worth citing at some length:

> the ground [*fond*] of the landscape rises up to the surface, inanimate objects are exhumed from the horizon and come each in turn to permeate the glaze of the windscreen, perspective becomes animated, the vanishing point becomes a point of attack sending forth its lines of projection on to the voyeur–voyageur, the objective of the continuum becomes a focal point that casts its rays on the dazzled observer, fascinated by the progression of landscapes. The generative axis of an apparent movement materializes suddenly through the speed of the machine, but this concretization is totally relative to the moment, for the object that hurls itself upon the layer of the windscreen will also be as quickly forgotten as perceived, stored away in the prop room, it will soon disappear in the rear window.
>
> (Virilio 2005a: 105)

This is a key example of the way, according to Virilio, 'speed metamorphoses appearances' (Virilio 2005a: 105). Interestingly, he once again deploys the language of painting and the psychology of form used in the forward to *Negative Horizon* (specifically in the reference to 'ground' or *fond* in French). The car traveller perceives the landscape as a background against which figures emerge or manifest themselves, a background which is not fixed, but which is itself mobile. Against this mobile horizon figures 'travel' as it were across the field of vision one after the other. If we normally think of depth vision in terms of a series of fixed lines which, as they recede into the distance, converge (the 'vanishing point' of classical perspective), we are presented here with a rather different experience. Where there should be a stable or immobile vanishing point there is a continuous emergence of lines of movement and forms ('a point of attack'). Where figures or forms placed along lines of perspective might normally remain fixed or be slowly enlarged as a perceiving body gradually approaches, there is rather a throwing or a hurling of them across the field of vision. This is an experience of 'dromoscopy', the car windscreen being the 'dromoscope', one which 'displays inanimate objects as if they were animated by a violent movement' (Virilio 2005a: 105). As an experience it demonstrates perfectly the way in which, for Virilio, speed is both a relation between phenomena and that which determines the truth of their 'sudden appearance' (*surgissement*). The constantly changing landscape is constituted as a field of appearance or vision only in the relative movements of the body and those of its perceived objects. The body hurtles forward, the objects, which would appear fixed if the body were stationary, are brought into the illusion of rapid motion. If those objects are themselves moving they will appear differently, depending on their relation to the trajectory of the vehicle-bound body. All this, perhaps, is stating nothing but the obvious. What we ignore, however, when we think of such an experience straightforwardly as merely rapid motion through space, is the properly *constitutive* role of speed in the structuration of the visual field.

This is the first sense in which space, for Virilio, is always a speed-space. The experience of dromoscopy, that is, of vision as structured or constituted in rapid motion, underlines the manner in which the space of vision is dependent upon the more or less rapid motion of the body in relation to its perceived objects. Yet Virilio also maintains that dromoscopy is, in certain respects, a decisively different experience from that of the body which might walk, jog or generally progress more slowly through its natural environment. The experience of things in the high-speed motion of the dromoscope not only shapes the way they appear but also alters our relationship to them. They can no longer be felt, be touched or encountered in their 'fixity of presence', since they appear to us only as objects hurtling past, as fleeting forms which begin to disappear in the very moment of their appearance. For Virilio this loss of fixity in relation to the presence of things is also a loss of their sensible reality and to that extent a kind of deception undergone by the traveller: 'Dromoscopy is, therefore, paradoxically *the wait for the coming of that which abides*: the trees that file past on the screen of the windshield [are] all substitutes for reality, these apparent movements are only simulacra' (Virilio 2005a: 115). Virilio uses the term 'simulacrum' to describe the fleeting nature of dromoscopic forms. A simulacrum is an imperfect or bad copy of an original, an unreal or vague semblance of that which it appears to be. The loss or diminution of presence to which the simulacral experience of speed gives rise will be explored more fully in the following chapter.

At this stage it need be noted only that dromoscopy reveals more clearly and decisively that space, that is, the phenomenal space of sensible appearance, is a speed-space. Speed as relative movement is, as it were, a form of mediation between things as they appear in any field of vision. It is the element in which the appearance of things takes place. This is true at perhaps a much more fundamental level when the second factor which shapes the 'dromosphere' of speed space is taken into account, that is, the speed of light which illuminates phenomena for perception or vision. In *Polar Inertia* Virilio gives his most extended account of the manner in which light is constitutive of the dromosphere, that is, the space of visibility as such. In this context he also uses phrases such as 'the light of speed' or the 'speed which lights'. Such phrases articulate a – perhaps rather singular – modification of what may more usually be understood as the 'speed of light'. Within the realm of physical science the speed of light is the universal constant which designates the speed at which light travels through a vacuum and is defined as being exactly 299,792,458 m per second. The light which permeates our environment or atmosphere, that which radiates down from the sky or which is emitted from light bulbs, cathode-ray tubes, neon signs etc., does not, of course, pass through a vacuum. Here more than ever one needs to be careful to differentiate the phenomenological register of Virilio's thinking from that of science, despite, or precisely because of, the fact that notions such as 'the light of speed' may be related to the scientifically determined constant of the 'speed of light'. The space of vision and perception is, in this context, a dromosphere, in so far as it is light, or, more precisely, the speed *of* light (that is, the speed which is proper or belongs to light) which makes things visible to us in the first instance. This allows Virilio in *Polar Inertia* to make the following claims: 'it is SPEED which lights up the universe of perceptible and measurable phenomena' or 'light remains the unique revealer of sensible appearances' (Virilio 2000d: 45, 55).

Once again this means that speed, in this case the speed of light, is both enabling and limiting. It is the condition of possibility for the visibility of phenomena but as such limits the manner in which they may appear. In order to understand this rather difficult conception a further example may be helpful. Throughout *Polar Inertia* Virilio makes explicit and regular reference to scientific thought and discovery and, in particular, to the theory of relativity given by Albert Einstein. His interest is specifically in the manner in which Einstein's insights altered the manner in which the physical universe was conceived, marking a break from the Newtonian view of the universe. Einstein's discovery of the universal constant C (the speed of light as it passes through a vacuum) altered the relation of any observer to perceivable phenomena and, famously of course, altered scientific conceptions of space and time (giving rise to Einsteinian space-time understood as a four-dimensional continuum of one temporal and three spatial co-ordinates in which any event or object can be located).

One of the consequences of this shift which is of particular interest to Virilio is the fact that any act of scientific observation within the physical universe can occur only in a temporally and spatially bound relation of the observer to the observed. An observation may yield different results depending on the relative positions of the perceiver and the perceived. (This is of particular significance with regard to the *movement* of both.) The optical observation of distant stellar objects is perhaps a familiar and easily accessible example of this. The further a telescope is able to view into the universe the further back in time it is able to see. As the universe expands so all the stellar and other objects within it get further away from the earth, that is, from the point of observation. Since the speed of light is a constant, and since the distances involved are so vast, the more distant the object the longer it has taken for the light it emits to reach the telescope. This means that the light we see from the sun may have taken around eight minutes to reach us and that we see the sun as it was eight minutes ago. The light from the most distant objects will have taken many billions of years to reach us and we are therefore able to see such objects as they were so many billions of years ago. This opens up the possibility that scientists may explore events of the early universe simply by developing the technical means to see further. Observation here is inseparable from the temporal and spatial interval which is marked by the relative positions of the seer and the seen. This example demonstrates the way in which, in the post-Einsteinian universe, the observer and the observed are always positioned relative to each other and the manner in which this relativity of observation is rooted in the constant of the speed of light which allows observation to occur. It is this discovery from within the realm of science which provides the grounding insight for

Virilio's conception of the 'dromosphere'. In *Polar Inertia* he defines this term in the following way: '"The DROMOSPHERE" [is] the sphere of speeds relative to that finite and absolute speed of light, the universal constant which determines the *cosmological* horizon, that is to say the cone of visibility of astronomical appearances' (Virilio 2000d: 45). The dromosphere then is 'the sphere of perception of the very reality of phenomena' (Virilio 2000d: 52) in so far as it is limited by the passage of light and therefore by the speed at which light travels. Virilio is insistent that it is speed which allows us to see, and all relative speeds, e.g. that of light as it passes through the atmosphere, that of opto-electronic waves which might transmit a television, satellite or digital image, are to be thought relative to the constant determined by the speed of light passing through a vacuum.

Particular care should be taken here to differentiate the manner in which Virilio shifts from the register of science and scientific theory (that of Einstein) to the phenomenological register which is preoccupied with immediate perception. As has been shown, Virilio does take from science the finding that the observation of phenomena is limited by the relative spatio-temporal positioning of the observer and the observed. He does so in order to highlight the importance of speed in the illumination of phenomenal appearance and develop his own phenomenological concept of the dromosphere. Yet his principal interest in *Polar Inertia* (and in other key works such as *The Vision Machine* and *The Information Bomb*) lies in the way in which new technologies such as television, live satellite broadcasts, video-surveillance or indeed the observation of minute or sub-atomic spaces, 'light up' the world in a different way and transform our (purely phenomenological) apprehension of space and time. So, if Virilio does refer to scientific theories, he does so in order to shift back into the dominant key of his phenomenological outlook.

It is this shift from one register into another which, no doubt, earned Virilio the condemnation of Alan Sokal and Jean Bricmont, who published a polemical and highly controversial book entitled *Intellectual Impostures* in 1998 (Sokal and Bricmont 1998). In the chapter devoted to Virilio they suggested that his references to science, specifically to Einstein's theory of relativity, to notions of space-time and to the basics of Newtonian physics, are 'confused' and 'fundamentally meaningless' (Sokal and Bricmont 1998: 159). Their engagement with Virilio is arguably symptomatic of their blindness to the philosophical contexts which underpin the thought of the various figures they criticize, a blindness which has been highlighted well by, among others, Colin Davis (Davis 2004: 27) and the American critic

Arkady Plotnitsky (Plotnitsky 2002: 112–13). As has been indicated, Virilio certainly does refer to scientific theories, and to Einsteinian relativity theory in particular. Yet, it has been emphasized, the dominant register of his writing is not scientific but phenomenological. He interrogates sense perception on the level of immediate appearances, a level which, according to the phenomenological perspective of Husserl, discussed in the last chapter, precedes the formal, mathematical abstraction of science. Without this key reference to phenomenology and to the interrogation of sense perception, Virilio's writing may appear confused and fundamentally meaningless to some, yet this is less a symptom of his abusive relation to scientific theory, and far more a result of the limited philosophical horizons of those who would attack him for such alleged abuses.

Sokal and Bricmont's criticism of Virilio not only reveals their lack of knowledge in relation to key features of his philosophical background but, more importantly, it makes them singularly unable to identify or interpret the shifts between the registers of scientific theory and of phenomenological description which have been identified here. When Virilio talks about 'speed-space', 'light-time' 'light of speed' he is specifically not referring to scientific concepts but is, once again, talking about the spatiality and temporality that we experience in our immediate perception of the world of sensible appearance. It has been argued here that Virilio's account of speed-space and the dromosphere need to be understood first in terms of the importance to the movement of objects in the constitution of any field of vision and secondly in terms of the speed (of light) which illuminates that field of vision in the first instance. It is from this dromological perspective that Virilio is able to address the impact of new (vehicular and communication) technologies on perception. In particular it is from this perspective that he is able to address the manner in which such technologies have come to transform our collective spatial and temporal experience.

LIGHT-TIME

Virilio's thinking of the dromosphere and speed-space is accompanied by an attempt to rethink the way in which temporal experience may be conceived. If, for Virilio, speed becomes the element or milieu in which the spatial world of perceptible phenomena appears to us, it also necessarily transforms the manner in which we may think of time. Necessarily because, according to the phenomenological account, perception always occurs as a lived experience in which spatiality and temporality are inseparably bound up each with the other. Within this context Virilio identifies a shift from what might be called 'chronological time' to 'light-time'. We all understand very easily our everyday understanding of temporal experience. We are situated in a present moment or a 'now' which we feel slipping away into a series of past moments and moving forward purposefully into a future moment or 'now'. This experience we translate easily into chronological time as measured by clocks in hours, minutes and seconds. From the phenomenological perspective this experience of time passing, or of duration, is intimately connected with the appearance of perceived objects, as Husserl makes clear in his *Thing and Space* lectures of 1907 (Husserl 1997: 55). According to Husserl the flow of sensory data which forms the basis of perceptible appearances has a tenseless ordering which becomes tensed only in the temporality of conscious experience. In our apprehension of the present we retain sensations of the immediate past just as we anticipate future sensations. Our experience of a present moment or 'now' and of time passing therefore occurs only on the basis of this retention of an immediate past and anticipation of a future possibility (what Husserl refers to as *protention*). What we think of as linear or objective time, that is, time as thought and measured by science, is, Husserl would argue, always secondary in nature, just as the conception of space as three extended dimensions is secondary in relation to our embodied experience of spatiality. For Virilio, once we begin to think of space as speed-space, or as a dromosphere 'lit up' by the light of speed, we need also to think this structure of duration and of chronological time in a subtly altered manner. In *Polar Inertia* he puts this in the following terms:

> From now on we need to associate the chronological 'movement' of past, present and future with phenomena of acceleration and deceleration . . . , the changes in speed which are allied to phenomena of lighting, to an exposure of the extension and duration of matter and to the light of day. . . . In effect, the order of (absolute) speed is an order of light in which the three classical tenses are reinterpreted in a system which is not exactly that of chronology.
>
> (Virilio 2000d: 38)

Time, Virilio asserts, should no longer be understood as an order of duration, of the succession of past, present and future moments, but should, rather, be understood as an order of 'exposure', that is, of the instant in which phenomena are lit up by, or exposed to, the light of speed. This new concept of a 'time of exposure' is perhaps one of Virilio's most difficult. The use of the term 'exposure' in photography may be helpful here. In this context it would be readily understood as the act of exposing photographic film to light in order to produce an image on the chemically sensitized surface of the film. The image produced results from the exact moment or instant in which light strikes the film (controlled by the shutter of the camera). Should the photosensitive film be exposed to light for too long or too little a period of time the image will not be clearly imprinted (being either over- or under-exposed). The existence of figures or forms in photographic images is clearly inseparable from this instantaneous quality of exposure. They do not communicate an experience of duration, since they cannot record either the flow of light which precedes the moment of exposure nor an anticipation of that which may follow. For Virilio light-time describes an experience of temporality in which phenomena are lit up in the manner of photographic exposure. We perceive sensible appearances in the instant of their exposure to light just as the photographic image is formed in the instant of its exposure as controlled by the camera shutter. This may seem rather counter-intuitive, since we do, after all, experience duration. States of boredom and waiting, for instance, remind us all too well of this. Virilio's point is perhaps that the experience of duration would not be possible if phenomena were not, in the first instance, exposed to light in the moment of their appearance. This means that the extensive nature of duration, that is, of time passing by in a structure of past, present, future, has as its prior condition the intensive experience of light-time as the time of exposure. Light-time is intensive rather than extensive because it is, as it were, only in the intensivity of the instant or moment of illumination that appearance occurs and does so as a field of temporally and spatially perceived forms. This, Virilio writes in *Polar Inertia*, is a time which is inextricably bound up with speed or with the speed-space of the dromoshpere because it is 'this time which *is exposed*, like space, to the light of the universal constant of speed' (Virilio 2000d: 53).

DROMOLOGY

For Virilio, then, terms such as dromosphere, speed-space and light-time are used within the context of a broader attempt to rethink temporal and spatial experience from the perspective of speed. Although he makes key references to scientific theories such as Einsteinian relativity, he does so in order to suggest ways in which such theories might allow, or provoke, the creation of new concepts, developed in a phenomenological register, and which relate, not to science, but to the realm of immediate perception. In this context scientific concepts such as Einsteinian 'space-time' give way to 'speed-space' or 'light-time', and the scientifically determined value of 'the universal constant of the speed of light' gives way to the 'constant universal light of speed'. There is a degree of linguistic playfulness in this alteration of terms, but it is a playfulness which needs to be taken very seriously if we are to understand the manner in which Virilio shifts between the registers of science and phenomenological description. Most importantly, the new terms or concepts he develops provide the basis for his wider interrogation of the impact of technologies upon individual or collective experience and upon social, political or military space. If dromology is a body of knowledge concerned with the manner in which speed determines or shapes the appearance of phenomena, then the dromosphere, speed-space and light-time are arguably the key concepts which give that body of knowledge coherence and a degree of theoretical unity and cohesion.

This is an important point to note because Virilio's discursive style or general mode of argumentation is not one of systematic exposition or logical deduction. On the contrary his writing can give the impression of having been written at great speed and with a large degree of spontaneity. In place of any systematic exposition the reader of Virilio's text is presented with a flow of anecdotes and insights, of concepts and references drawn from extremely diverse areas of knowledge. His texts are woven from a vast array of historical and factual detail, peppered with repeated citations of politicians, critics and military figures: Clausewitz, Sun Tzu, a 1960s mayor of Philedelphia speaking after street riots, Churchill, Hitler and many others. Yet, if, on the first reading, Virilio's texts can appear confusing or disorientating, any persistent and careful reader will soon realize that there is some degree of method in his apparently haphazard approach. Rather than the step-by-step development of an argument Virilio's thinking proceeds as an accumulation of references, facts, insights and theoretical interrogation. This cumulative aspect of his writing is important to note, since it is only in the repetition of key terms or of the same point made in different contexts that it gains a degree of unity and cohesion. An example drawn from *Open Sky* may help to illustrate the nature of Virilio's discursive style.

In the following passage he is discussing the effect that the use of telescopes and radio telescopes in astronomy has had on our general ways of viewing the universe. In particular Virilio is interested in the manner in which different ways of viewing the cosmos have given rise to competing theories, for instance the notion of a continually expanding and contracting universe which, historically, has rivalled the Big Bang theory (that is, the notion that the universe was born in an original cosmic explosion of matter). The passage occurs in the chapter entitled 'Large-scale optics' at the end of the first part of *Open Sky*. (The term 'Large-scale optics' will be discussed more fully in the following chapter.) The terminology used here and the perspective adopted are a clear repetition of the terms and theoretical insights developed in earlier works such as *Negative Horizon* and *Polar Inertia*:

> Magnification, optical diminution [*Grandissement, rapetissement optique*], Doppler effect of the red shift observed in the spectrum of the galaxies, other denominations of acceleration and deceleration of appearances, in which the DROMOSHPERE – the light of speed – *literally lights up perceptible reality*, a reality whose STEREOSCOPIC RELIEF already provokes a number of perceptual disorders of which it will, it appears, be necessary finally to take note, since the very notion of 'physical proximity' risks soon to be radically altered. The LARGE-SCALE OPTICS which permits a testing of the most vast astronomical distance, contributing also but inversely to the invalidation of the closest physical proximity.
>
> (Virilio 1997a: 43–4)

Looking at the strictly stylistic aspects of this passage, rather than at the content, we might immediately note a common characteristic of Virilio's writing, namely his tendency to emphasize key words or phrases, either by placing them in capital letters or by italicizing them. He tends to capitalize those terms which occupy a key place in his theoretical lexicon and which are therefore likely to appear often across a range of his texts (e.g. 'DROMOSPHERE' and 'LARGE-SCALE OPTICS' above). He also capitalizes those terms to which, in a more local manner, he wishes specifically to draw our attention (e.g. 'STEREOSCOPIC RELIEF'). The frequent use of italics underlines the importance of key elements in a sentence but also gives a more generally emphatic quality to his writing. It might also be noted that, in the original French of the passage above, Virilio frequently omits the use of indefinite and definite articles 'a' and 'the' (e.g. 'Magnification, optical diminution, Doppler effect', 'light of speed'). This gives his writing a telegraphic quality, that is, a sense of abruptness but also one which suggests a heightened speed of communication or passage of the text. Taken together these aspects are typical of the style of Virilio's writing: the capitalized terms and italicized phrases give an almost dramatic or explosive quality to a text which, in the frequent omission of articles and the rapid passage of one thought or insight to another, appears as the very linguistic embodiment of the thought of speed. It is as if the alteration in perception and understanding to which, according to Virilio, the experience of speed gives rise, is itself embodied in the fabric of his written style. Yet at the same time this writing is underpinned by a striking continuity both in its use of specific terms and in the sameness of its underlying preoccupations. It is clear for instance that, in the passage cited above, concepts developed at some length in *Polar Inertia* and *Negative Horizon* occupy a central place (dromosphere, light of speed). There is also once again a shifting between the registers of scientific theory (in the reference to cosmology) and that of perception (in the references to 'appearances', 'perceptual disorders' and to the spatial experience of proximity and distance).

Such a passage makes little sense if the reader does not attend closely both to the manner in which it is written, that is, to its telegraphic style, the use of capitals and italics, and to the manner in which this style reflects or embodies the dominant concern with speed which permeates all of Virilio's writing. Such passages are also likely to be misunderstood if they are read simply as a series of stand-alone propositions or factual statements. As was argued at the end of the preceding chapter, Virilio's work aims to challenge received ways of seeing and understanding the world. In order to do this he develops new terms and concepts or transforms existing ones. It is only in the context of a repeated and cumulative use of certain neologisms across a number of texts that many of his statements make sense or carry with them a coherent and persuasive force.

Dromology, then, as a body of knowledge concerned with the way in which speed shapes or determines the appearance of phenomena, is grounded in a work of conceptual re-figuration and of stylistic innovation which takes speed as its guiding motif. The concepts of dromosphere, speed-space and light-time discussed here, *and* Virilio's discursive style, all are inspired by a thinking which aims to make of speed the element or milieu in which experience, meaning and understanding unfold. Dromology is, as Virilio puts it: 'a hidden science (that of speed), both a logistical comple-ment and supplement to the science of life' (Virilio 2005a: 132). It should not be confused with the science of life, with physical or natural science, rather it has its own specific and specifically demarcated areas of concern, its own discursive method and manner of proceeding. In *Negative Horizon* Virilio notes: 'it is transports and transmissions that command production, to the point that dromology today appears like a science whose theories take the forms of vehicles' (Virilio 2005a: 132). For Virilio a way of writing is a way of seeing, and vision, it has been shown, is always shaped by a vector of movement or by a relative positioning of the seer and the seen, by a lighting up in the 'light of speed'. A vehicle here is a means of shaping or directing a vector of movement or a relation of seeing. It can be the dromoscope of a train or car, a manner of writing or, as will become clear, a television screen, a computer terminal or video surveillance device. It is in this notion of the vehicle that Virilio address one of the major themes or concerns of dromology: the becoming virtual or desertification of lived embodied experience.

SUMMARY

The question of speed runs throughout Virilio's work and his writing as a whole can be thought of as a practice of 'dromology'. Dromology should be understood as a body of knowledge which concerns itself with speed and with the way in which speed determines or limits the appearance of phenomena. Dromology as a body of knowledge is underpinned by a number of key concepts relating to speed, most importantly 'speed space', the 'dromosphere' and 'light-time'. Speed-space refers to a dimension of primordial spatial experience which is defined by relative movements and by the relative or changing speeds of those movements. The dromosphere describes the sphere of speeds relative to the speed of light and as such represents the space of visibility or appearance itself in so far as it is both illuminated and limited by the passage of light. Light-time describes an experience of temporality determined by the manner in which phenomena are illuminated in the instant of their exposure to light. Light-time is not the extensive duration of past, present and future but is 'intensive' in so far as it is constituted in the instant in which phenomena are exposed to light and made visible as such. Care needs to be taken to differentiate Virilio's dromological concepts from scientific concepts. Virilio's dromological discourse is also written in a singular style which adapts itself to the theoretical perspective of dromology more generally.

3

VIRTUALIZATION

Vehicles, vision machines and virtual presence

The last chapter showed that Virilio's writing not only describes the manner in which speed shapes perception, but that it also develops new concepts and discursive strategies. These respond to the transformation in understanding to which the 'dromological' perspective gives rise. This chapter will examine Virilio's contention that the accelerated speeds of transmission and communication afforded by modern technologies lead to a loss of immediate presence and a diminution of lived embodied experience. This is a theme which runs throughout Virilio's writing from the mid-1970s through to the present day and which is often expressed in apocalyptic or catastrophic terms. In certain respects his analysis is reminiscent of the perspective elaborated by the Italian Futurists who celebrated technologies of speed in the early twentieth century. In 'The Founding Manifesto of Futurism' (1909) F. W. Marinetti (1876–1944) asserted that modernity could be defined as an age of speed and proclaimed: 'Time and Space died yesterday. We already live in the absolute, because we have created eternal, omnipresent speed' (Apollonio 1973: 22). Yet far from celebrating speed in the manner of Marinetti, Virilio's dromology offers a sustained account of its negative impact on the shaping of perception and of social or political space. The ability to traverse the world at high speed, either via the accelerated rapidity of transports or in the instantaneity of telecommunication, is viewed in terms of a negation of the space, volume or extension of the world. This is clear from a comment Virilio makes in one of his earliest full-length works, *The Insecurity of Territory* (*L'Insécurité du territoire*): 'From now on all is extreme, the END of the world can be felt in this situation which results from the super-conductibility of milieus just as it does from the hyper-communicability of means' (Virilio 1993: 264). This is a constant refrain throughout Virilio's writing, one which is repeated in very similar terms in one of his most recent works, *City of Panic*: 'the slow miniaturisation of our terrestrial habitat's proportions, through the constant acceleration of all paths, is an insidious form of the *desertification of the world*' (Virilio 2005b: 113). It reflects Virilio's general contention that a world of accelerated speeds is one in which there is: 'a decline in existence', a 'crisis of dimensions and of representation' (Virilio 1991b: 37, 50), or a world which is entering its old age (Virilio 2000d: 76).

As was indicated in the first chapter, it is easy to take catastrophist statements such as these entirely at face value and to assume that Virilio's discourse on technologies of speed is nothing other than negative or pessimistic. It has also been suggested, however, that his writing has a performative aspect: it seeks to reveal the world to us in a different almost provocative way, to expose aspects of technological development which might otherwise remain hidden and to provide new concepts and tools of understanding. Rather than their apocalyptic or catastrophic tone, what is perhaps most interesting about the comments cited above is the manner in which means of transport and means of communication become almost interchangeable: the 'super-conductibility of milieus' effected by high-speed travel is in no way different from the 'hyper-communicability of means' afforded by modern communications. This may appear to be a rather strange conflation of divergent experiences. According to our everyday way of thinking the ability to move rapidly through space by means of high-speed transport is very different from our ability to communicate quasi-instantaneously over vast distance by means of modern telecommunications. In the first case we get somewhere else more or less quickly in the second we remain very much fixed where we are. Yet this everyday understanding ignores what is most crucial to Virilio's dromological perspective: that speed is not a phenomenon itself but rather a relation between phenomena. From this perspective there is, of course, an important difference between being in rapid motion through space or being stationary but able to see or hear at a distance. Yet what is fundamentally important is that the temporal and spatial relationship between the seer and the seen has been altered by a specific speed of transmission (the landscape fleeting past, the presence of an image on screen, near yet distant, visible yet untouchable). In *Negative Horizon* Virilio puts this in the following terms:

henceforth [there is] only one mediation, not that of the vector, of the vehicle, but that of its speed; between the audiovisual media and the automobile (that is the dromovisual), there is no difference; *speed machines*, they both give rise to mediation through the production of speed.

(Virilio 2005a: 116)

High speed transport and instantaneous or quasi-instantaneous telecommunication are different only in so far as they are different aspects of the same phenomenon, that is dromoscopy or vision as mediated by speed. At the very end of the last chapter it was suggested that, for Virilio, a vehicle is not simply a means of automated transport, rather it is, in a much broader sense, a means of seeing or of articulating vision in a specific vector and speed of transmission. The apocalyptic tone of Virilio's writing can only be approached or understood, judged or criticized, from the perspective of the 'speed machine', whether it be a mode of transport or a means of communication. More specifically his catastrophist pronouncements are rooted in his analysis of the impact of speed machines on the fundamentals of perception and on the appearance of sensible reality.

VIRTUAL PRESENCE

As has been indicated, the 'becoming virtual' of perceptual experience is one of the most persistent and repeated themes of Virilio's work. In light of this it would be impossible to treat it exhaustively within the space of a short chapter. What follows, then, will focus primarily on Virilio's references to the virtualization of experience in three major works: *The Lost Dimension, The Vision Machine* and *Polar Inertia*. Previous chapters, it may be recalled, have shown the way in which, according to the phenomenological perspective which Virilio adopts, the 'presence' of lived experience is always viewed in terms of a primary spatiality and temporality which are constituted in, or along with, the appearance of phenomena to perception. What might be called 'actual presence', that is, the apparent immediacy of sensible objects within a field of vision and accessible to touch, usage or manipulation, can only be thought on the basis of this primary situatedness of the perceiving body.

Virilio's contention is that speed machines fundamentally alter the way in which we perceive. They alter the different spatial and temporal elements constitutive of 'actual presence' and therefore restructure our relation to the world of sensible appearance. This alteration in perception has already been described, in preliminary fashion, in the examples of train and car travel given in the preceding chapters. Yet the impact of speed machines is, according to Virilio, in no way limited to the dromoscopic experience of rapid or high-speed travel. Far more importantly, he is concerned with the way in which a society permeated with speed machines leads to what is termed a 'teletopological' structuring of perception. This, again, is a neologism coined by Virilio himself and derives from a double root: from the Greek *tele*, meaning distant or far (as in *television* or *tele*communication), and from the Greek *topos*, meaning place or common place. If the topological relates to the reality of a given place, its historical and geological form, then the 'teletopological' would relate to the reality of a place or form as viewed from a distance. In *The Vision Machine* Virilio describes this alteration in the structuring of actual presence in the following terms, once again referring to Merleau-Ponty:

> All that I see is, in principle, within my reach (at least within the reach of my gaze), it is registered on the map of what 'I can do'. In this important phrase, Merleau-Ponty precisely describes that which is ruined by a teletopology which has become ordinary. The essentials of what I see are no longer, in effect or in principle, within my reach and even if it is within reach of my gaze it is no longer necessarily inscribed on the map of what 'I can do'.
>
> (Virilio 1994b: 7)

The notion of the 'I can' can be found in the work of both Husserl and Merleau-Ponty and describes once again the manner in which perception is rooted in the situated possibilities and orientation of the physical body. Virilio is suggesting that 'teletopology' leads to a separation of what is perceived in any visual field and the ability of our body to touch, use or manipulate that which is perceived. This may seem a rather complex way of referring to a state of affairs which is quite straightforward or obvious: the televised image of a satellite broadcast or the figures shown on a screen during, say, a live video conference, can be viewed, they are intelligible as visible images or figures, but they cannot be touched, approached or physically engaged with. Yet Virilio is, as always, inviting us to look more closely at this experience and to think about what might be at stake in the separation of the sensible and the intelligible to which such images give rise. For his part he sees at work a loss or a reduction in the richness or density of sensible experience. In *Negative Horizon* he puts this in the following terms, claiming that it is as if 'speed now attacks the very density of masses, as if the objective had suddenly become the durability and thickness of the physical body as a whole' (Virilio 2005a: 125–6). It is to this loss of density, durability and thickness of physical bodies that Virilio refers when he talks of teletopology or of virtual as opposed to actual presence.

This concern is most clearly reflected in his treatment of the cinematic image and what he comes to term the 'aesthetic of disappearance'. The example of the cinematic image can offer a helpful means of understanding what exactly is at stake for Virilio when he speaks of virtual presence. In speaking about cinema he draws a distinction between an 'aesthetic of appearance' on the one hand and an 'aesthetic of disappearance' on the other. The former describes the manner in which we encounter works of art such as painting or sculpture, the latter the manner in which we view the images of film. Virilio is interested in the way in which a sculpture or painting appears as a stable form which persists through time by virtue of its materiality. For example, the Venus de Milo or the Mona Lisa both remain as they are, they remain unique and durable because of the stone, canvas, paints and pigments from which they are made. The manner in which the film image appears is quite different. No such stability exists, since its material support is not the fixity of carved stone, paint or pigment but rather the rapid movement of celluloid passed in front of a projection lamp. As viewers of film we have a sense of continuity from one passing image to the other and therefore an experience of a moving image. Virilio explains the illusion of movement given to us by the cinematic image by reference to the now outdated theory of 'retinal persistence'. This theory was once used by scientists to explain why we see a rapid succession of still images as a moving image. The assumption was that visual stimuli were stored in the memory for a few hundred milliseconds after they had disappeared and that this retention allowed the intervals of darkness between individual film images to be filled in. Each new visual stimulus would register on the eye before the preceding visual impression had entirely passed and would thus give rise to a sense of continuity and therefore of movement. The illusion of movement given by film is nowadays explained with reference to what is known as the 'phi effect'. It is now thought that certain neurons exist in the retina which specialize in detecting movement and that it is due to these, and not the retention of past visual stimuli, that a succession of still images can appear to give an image in motion. The exact mechanism by which the illusion of motion, or the phi effect, occurs is less important for Virilio than the fact that what was a stable, material presence in sculpture or painting gives way to an unstable, fleeting presence in the cinematic image. The duration of the cinema image is that of its passing or disappearance.

This shift from an aesthetic of appearance to one of disappearance is described in *The Lost Dimension* in the following terms:

> From the aesthetic of appearance of a *stable image*, present by virtue of its static form, to the aesthetic of disappearance of an *unstable image* present by virtue of its (cinematic, cinematographic . . .) flight, we have experienced a great transmutation of representations. The emergence of forms, of volumes destined to persist in the duration of their material support has been succeeded by images whose sole duration is that of retinal persistence.
>
> (Virilio 1991a: 25–6)

What is at stake here is not simply a difference in the way we view different types of art but rather modes or ways of seeing which can begin to structure our more generalized habits of perception in new and perhaps unforeseen or indiscernible ways. With the advent of cinema, the argument runs, new possibilities of collectively experiencing the world emerge. For Virilio an aesthetic of disappearance is radically different in so far as visible images are constituted in the material absence of the object which is represented but, most importantly, because the very fleeting nature of their appearance structures the temporality of perception differently. In *The Vision Machine* this is discussed in terms of the different process by which the cinematic image is 'objectivized', that is, actualized as a visible figure or form:

> The problem of the objectivization of the image is not [in film] posed in relation to any *surface-support* of paper or celluloid, that is, with reference to a space of material reference, but rather in relation to time, *to this time of exposition which* allows or edits seeing.
>
> (Virilio 1994b: 61)

This formulation directly recalls the thinking of light-time discussed in the preceding chapter. What is at stake in the shift Virilio identifies from an aesthetic of appearance to an aesthetic of disappearance is a loss of spatial and material reference in favour of a dominant reference to a temporal dimension of exposure. A temporal structure of duration (that of the material stability and persistence of stone, canvas, paint etc.) gives way to one in which the appearing form appears only in the instant in which it is 'lit up' or exposed to light (as emitted by the projector) and indeed appears only in an instant which is also that of its continual disappearance. Cinema, then, gives us an image of the world of sensible appearances in which spatiality and temporality are transformed: spatial and material extension are lost in favour of what Virilio terms an 'intensivity' of a temporality of exposure.

One way of putting this would be to say that the cinematic image offers a different kind of window on the world. In *The Aesthetics of Disappearance* Virilio talks at some length of the way in which collective ways of viewing were transformed in the late nineteenth and early twentieth centuries by the advent of cinema halls. By way of newsreels or other footage the reality of global space could be seen as never before by millions of people. The motorized passage of celluloid in front of a projection lamp represents, therefore, nothing other than a different way of 'lighting' the world, that is, of making it accessible to vision and therefore to conscious apprehension. In this context Virilio speaks of the 'appearance of the motor' and here a double meaning can perhaps be inferred: motorized film-projection appears or emerges as a technology of viewing but it also has a mode of appearance which belongs or which is proper to it: 'With the appearance of the motor, another sun has risen, radically changing sight; its manner of giving light will rapidly alter all life' (Virilio 1991b: 50). On one level this alteration in life is quite straightforwardly related to social habit: the gathering together of masses of people in a darkened room to view a film is different from a gathering in a church or theatre. Where the latter offer a sacred ritual or theatrical performance involving actually present bodies (priests or actors), the former is a spectacle of light only, one in which, Virilio says, 'false constellations shine in an absorbent planetarium blue' and in which the spectators themselves have become 'fluorescent, as they also emit a mysterious glimmering light' (Virilio 1991b: 59). Within this spectacle of light the spaces of the world can be made present in their very absence, the speed and fleeting movement of the images of film liberate vision from the constraints of distance, of time and space. With the advent of the cinema hall:

> Everything took place within the multitude *of the luminous viewers* of a communal effusion which suddenly became a transmutation of all species, a moment of inertia where everything is already there in the *false*

day of an escape velocity of light which effectively liberates us from the need to travel in favour of the attentive impatience for a world which now constantly arrives and for which we now constantly wait.

(Virilio 1991b: 59)

This is a way of viewing the world in which the intervals of time and space which might separate say an audience in the East End of London from the Taj Mahal in India are annihilated in favour of a seeing at a distance, literally a tele-vision, which negates the need to depart or to travel in order then to see, and does so in favour of an arrival of a visible image when no departure has ever occurred. The notion of 'false day' plays a key role in Virilio's account of virtual presence. He is interested in the way different technologies over the centuries have allowed humans to light up the world differently. In order to supplement the light of the solar day we have used candles, torches, lamps and then finally electrically powered sources (light bulbs, neon tubes etc.). The cinema image, as a 'window on the world' which abolishes the temporal and spatial intervals which separate us from distant visible forms, marks a decisive shift beyond these various means of supplementing the solar day towards an alternate structure of vision. Here, it is not the reflection of light emitted from a direct source which 'lights up' visible forms, rather it is the passage of light as mediated by the rapid motion of film which gives, as it were, an indirectly illuminated visible form, one which is present by virtue of its absence, one whose appearance is predicated on its very disappearance.

The aesthetic of disappearance of the cinema image and the impact it has on both the temporality and the spatiality of seeing is perceived by Virilio to be a precursor to the contemporary world of television and modern media more generally. If cinema represents the dawn of a false day which begins to exist alongside the solar day, then television and contemporary media represent the light of that false day risen to its highest point. Arguably the 'daylight' of television is even further removed from presence than that emitted by the film projector. It could be argued that the images of film have some direct relation to the figures or forms they portray, since the light reflected off those figures or forms has passed *directly* from the object to the photosensitive surface of the celluloid. This might imply some, albeit virtual, trace of the material presence of the represented object. With television or other forms of electronic or digital transmission this is no longer the case. Light reflected from the form which is to be televised is converted into electrical pulses and only then reconverted into a visible image on the screen of the television itself. This, as will become clear, is what Virilio comes to call 'wave optics'. Here Virilio is once again primarily interested in the way in which the *false day* of the electronic image restructures the temporality and spatiality governing the perception of visible forms. In *The Lost Dimension* he explicitly compares television to the window of a house:

> ever since we open not just our curtains but also turn on the television, the light of day has been modified: to the solar day of astronomy, the uncertain day of candlelight, to electric light, is now added an *electronic false day* whose calendar is solely that of 'commutations' of information without any relation to real time. In this way a time which is instantaneously *exposed* succeeds the time which *passes* of chronology and history.
>
> (Virilio 1991a: 14)

In the light of comments such as these it would appear that the notion of 'light-time' discussed in the preceding chapter is not just a new dromological concept which attempts to rethink the nature of time from the perspective of speed. Light-time is also the lived temporality of perceptual experience as it is mediated by the speed machines of cinema, television and digital media. It is the time of the false day of electronic tele-images. A principal concern within Virilio's account of virtual presence is that cinema and now contemporary media have effected a shift from the spatial and the extensive (the spatiality of bodily experience, the extensivity of temporal duration) to the temporal and the intensive (the exposure of light-time and the intensivity of the exposed instant).

Virilio is seeking to describe nothing other than a generalized transformation, or what he has called a transmutation, of collective ways of seeing and representing. This transformation can be directly attributed to the advent of cinema, of television and of other digital media which allow for perception at a distance to occur. If we think of film, television and other media simply as forms of representation of a straightforwardly given pre-existing reality, then, Virilio would argue, we miss or pass over the decisive ways in which they reveal or constitute the appearance of the world in a fundamentally different manner. The more our collective social and cultural experience is saturated with these speed machines or vehicles of perception the greater the impact they are likely to have on our general habits of apprehending and conceiving reality. Once again Virilio identifies within our collective experience of contemporary media a gradual loss of the richness and diversity offered by immediate sensory perception: 'The increasing disequilibrium between direct information and indirect information, itself a result of diverse means of communication, tends excessively to privilege mediatized information to the detriment of that of the senses; the reality effect, it seems, supplants immediate reality' (Virilio 1991a: 24). The distinction Virilio draws here between the reality effect on the one hand and 'immediate reality' on the other is one which, he argues, is becoming increasingly confused or blurred the more our experience of the world is mediated through the false day of television and other media. On one level this might mean simply that we tend to 'believe what we see' when it comes to viewing information about the world as it is relayed to us via television and other broadcast media. One could respond to this by arguing that viewers of, say, television or other news are capable of a great deal of scepticism and cynicism and do not necessarily or always give great credence to the 'reality effect' produced by electronic media. Yet, as always, Virilio's argument relates less to the range of possible responses to the *content* of what we might see or absorb and more to the mode, structure or manner of its appearance. Whether we are more or less sceptical about what we see is less important than the fact that we are being exposed to a different manner of structuring perception and therefore our apprehension of sensible reality. Virilio puts this in the following terms:

> Henceforth we are present at (either a live or recorded) COPRODUCTION of sensible reality where direct and mediatized perceptions are mixed together in order to give an instantaneous representation of space, of the surrounding milieu. The interval between the reality of distances (of time and space) and the distancing of diverse (video graphic or info graphic) representations is abolished.
>
> (Virilio 1991a: 30–1)

It is the blending together of direct and mediatized perception which, for Virilio, provides an insidious mix which blinds us to the specific manner in which the world arrives to us in the speed machines of modern media. If, for instance, we are sitting in a living room watching a news item on the television relating, say, to an explosion in the Middle East, our visual and tactile field is composed by a number of diverse elements: the more or less comfortable upholstery of our chair or settee, the familiarity of our immediate surroundings (carpets, furniture, overhead lighting etc.) and the luminescent screen of the television, which gives us an image at once in a relation of close proximity (the screen is likely to be only a few metres away) and in a relation of distance (the image itself arrives more or less instantaneously from a far removed location). The impression of proximity offered by the tele-visual image is, of course, entirely false. Yet arguably the viewing of this 'other window' on the world becomes so ingrained in our habits of perception that we take the images it offers as much for granted as we do those appearances immediately surrounding us. We fail to discern or properly apprehend that, within the tele-image, distance prevails over proximity, the time of transmission prevails over the spatial materiality of sensible presence, and, above all, what is present is so only in its absence.

This is a phenomenon that Virilio comes to call 'tele-presence'. Arguably the general account of the virtualization of experience that is given in works such as *The Lost Dimension*, *The Vision Machine* and *Polar Inertia* relies on the idea of a generalizing of tele-presence effected by the speed machines of modern communications and digital or broadcast media. In *The Lost Dimension* Virilio sums this up in the following terms:

> An indirect and mediatized reception succeeds the instant of the direct perception of objects, surfaces and volumes (natural or constructed), in an interface which escapes daily duration and the calendar of the everyday. Let us delude ourselves no longer: we will never be close to televisual proximity, *the media are not our contemporaries*; today we are living in an ever increasing gap between the promptness of their retransmission and out ability to seize, to measure, the present instant.
> (Virilio 1991a: 84)

From the aesthetic of disappearance of cinema through to the telepresence of the modern media this loss of 'direct perception of objects, surfaces and volumes' provides the guiding thread and unifying principle of Virilio's account of the virtualization of collective experience. In each case speed and relative speeds of transmission (of the film reel past the projector lamp, of the instantaneous transfer of electronic or digital data) transform perception by abolishing spatial and material determinants in favour of a mode of appearing in which the temporality of exposure and the virtuality of telepresence come to dominate.

VISION MACHINES

If Virilio's account of virtualization and telepresence relies heavily on the notion of 'speed machines', it also relies on the notion of the 'vision machine'. A vision machine may best be described as a technical prosthesis (that is, an artificial device that replaces or supplements a normal bodily function) which allows us to alter or extend the manner in which we see. Virilio, albeit in a characteristically unsystematic manner, offers a speculative history of the development of vision machines from the Renaissance onwards. Central to this account, and to the notion of the vision machine more generally, is his use of the term 'transparency'. We would normally understand transparency as the possibility of perceiving rays of light through a particular substance. Virilio gives the following definitions in *Polar Inertia*: 'transparency is "that which lets light easily pass through", or alternatively: "that which allows objects to be clearly distinguished through its very density (as with glass, for example)"' (Virilio 2000d: 55). In this context phenomena and the world of sensible appearances more generally are 'lit up' or made accessible to vision in so far as light passes through a transparent medium. In the first place this medium is simply the earth's atmosphere itself: that through which light passes in order to illuminate landscapes, horizons and natural or man-made architectures. According to Virilio human history is marked by the invention of artificial media which supplement or transform this fundamental transparency offered by terrestrial space and its atmosphere.

This is a history which begins with the invention of glass and culminates with opto-electronics, as Virilio indicates, again in *Polar Inertia*, referring specifically to television:

> The transparency of space, the transparency of the horizon of travel, of our itinerary across the world is succeeded by this *cathodic transparency* which is nothing other than the perfect extension of the invention of glass four thousand years ago; an extension of the 'window', that enigmatic object which nevertheless marks the history of urban architecture, from the Middle Ages to the present day, or more exactly, to the recent invention of the *electronic window*, that last horizon of our journeys.
>
> (Virilio 2000d: 18–19)

This comment gives some indication as to why, as was discussed earlier, Virilio refers to television as another kind of 'window' on the world. He is invoking a history in which the original transparency of space is supplemented by that of glass in a way which allows a transformation in the possibilities of architectural and urban development. The invention of the glass window makes possible both the advent of new ways of constructing dwellings and a new medium through which the world can be viewed. The impact of this innovation in the nature of transparency is felt primarily within the area of the construction and organization of urban space and living space more generally. In this passage from the natural transparency of the earth's atmosphere to the 'cathodic transparency' of modern televisual media the next key moment of innovation is, according to Virilio, the invention of optical technologies in the Renaissance and, in particular, the invention of the telescope. Where the glass window is seen to make a wide-reaching impact on urban architecture and design, the telescope here transforms, in a decisive manner, fundamental possibilities of perception and with this fundamental ways of apprehending and knowing the physical universe. The amplifying powers of telescopic lenses inaugurate an entirely new mode of transparency as Virilio indicates towards the beginning of *The Vision Machine*:

> The very model of visual prostheses, the telescope projects an image of a world outside our reach and with that a different way of moving through the world; the *logistics of perception* inaugurates an unknown transfer of the gaze, it creates the telescoping of the near and the far, a *phenomenon of acceleration* which abolishes our apprehension of distances and dimensions.
>
> More than a return to antiquity, the Renaissance appears today as the emergence of a period in which all intervals were traversed, a morphological effraction which immediately affects the reality effect.
>
> (Virilio 1994b: 4)

With the invention of the telescope the origin of telepresence can be located historically and it should be clear from this that, for Virilio, the transformation of spatial and temporal perception effected by different technologies is by no means purely a product of late nineteenth and twentieth-century innovations. He does not, of course, suggest that prior to a certain specific historical moment or watershed of modernity we were somehow without technology. Rather, within the context of the speculative history of 'transparency' given, Virilio suggests that the optical technologies of the Renaissance and early modern period mark an inaugural moment in the development of vision machines. The transparency offered by the telescopic lens (as opposed to that offered by the atmosphere or the window) marks the first stage in the restructuring of spatial perception that modern vision machines have brought about. This development from straightforwardly transparent glass to the magnifying transparency of the telescopic lens culminates in the creation of contemporary technologies which permit visual perception through the transmission of radio waves or electronic pulses. This, Virilio contends, is yet again an entirely new order of transparency, since light does not pass directly through a material to permit vision (that is, the glass of the window or lens). Rather, light rays are converted into another form of energy in order then to be reconverted into light so that visual perception can occur. This new order of transparency implies a shift from direct to indirect seeing, since light no longer passes from its source through the transparent medium and then to the eye, but rather passes from the source and then indirectly to the eye via radio or electronic transmission. Virilio suggests the shift from direct to indirect transparency implies also a shift from a passive to an active optics:

> the surpassing of the direct transparency of materials is due, in the first instance, to the emergence of a new optics: an *active* optics which is the product of the recent development of opto-electronics and radio-electric viewing and works to the detriment of the former supremacy enjoyed by the *passive* optics of telescopic lenses, microscopes or recording cameras. To put it another way, we have witnessed the effective introduction of a *wave optics* [*optique ondulatoire*] alongside, exactly alongside, classical geometrical optics.
>
> (Virilio 2000d: 56)

What this suggests is that, for Virilio, the impact of vision machines on perception lies not simply in the way in which they alter our relation to space and spatial determination. It is not simply that things which are distant can, through telescopic or televisual seeing, be perceived as immediately present in a way which abolishes the normal distinction between near and far. What is at stake is the very medium in which the forms of sensible appearance become visible to us and, along with this, the categories of presence and absence, appearance and disappearance. Like the 'aesthetics of disappearance' inaugurated by the advent of cinema, the indirect, active transparency of wave optics alters the very the manner in which visible forms *are*. In this sense the telepresence of modern media discussed earlier in this chapter is not simply a 'presence at a distance', that is to say, a plenitude of being which, existing at a distance, is then brought near. Telepresence implies a virtuality of 'being there' which is neither presence nor absence strictly speaking, a virtuality which impinges on what might call the ontological status of telepresent forms. Put more simply, wave optics alters the being of sensible appearances.

This alteration in the being or substance of visible forms, when taken together with the transformation in spatial determinations that wave optics also effects, has, according to Virilio's account, far-reaching consequences. Transparency, it should be recalled, is a both a medium and a horizon of perception. Arguably the fundamental horizons which determine the way we view the visible world cannot be separated from the manner in which forms of knowledge develop and therefore from our wider understanding of the physical universe. Alfred Crosby, for example, has argued convincingly that the rise of optical technologies in the Renaissance exerted a decisive influence on the development of the scientific world view and the global dominance of Western culture more generally (Crosby 1997). Edmund Husserl also argued in his late work of the 1930s, *The Crisis in European Sciences and Transcendental Phenomenology*, that Galileo's innovations in astronomy (made possible by the telescope) were a foundational moment in the rise of modern science and, in particular, were foundational for its geometrical and mathematical approach to the world of phenomena (Husserl 1970). What this suggests is that the shift from the geometrical optics of the Renaissance to the wave optics of contemporary technologies would have the potential to restructure, not just perception, but the very building blocks of the way in which we understand the physical universe. The 'morphological effraction' which occurs in perception mediated by vision machines and 'which immediately affects the reality effect' (Virilio 1994b: 4) has, for Virilio, the potential to transform almost every aspect of the way we experience the world and come to know it.

What is at stake then in the history of vision machines and in their recent proliferation in the wave optics of the contemporary media is not just spatial and temporal perception but with this the basic building blocks of knowledge and changing character of human consciousness more generally. Earlier it was shown how Virilio, in *The Vision Machine*, cited Merleau-Ponty to suggest the way in which the teletopological structuring of perception undermined certain basic elements of bodily possibility. The visible forms of telepresence, Virilio maintained, are not inscribed upon the map of what 'I can do' (Virilio 1994b: 7), they are in a crucial way out of reach and so the relation of the body to the world of sensible appearances is radically altered. In *Phenomenology of Perception* Merleau-Ponty cites unpublished work by Husserl affirming that: 'Consciousness is in the first place not a matter of "I think that" but of "I can"' (Merleau-Ponty 2002: 137). Here Merleau-Ponty is clearly arguing against the model of consciousness posited by René Descartes (1596–1650), who, in his famous 'I think therefore I am', sought to ground thought in the immediate self-presence of a rational ego (Descartes: 1999). If one follows this phenomenological strand of thinking about bodily possibilities in the way that Virilio does, it becomes more or less inevitable that the telepresence and the teletopological structuring of perception permitted by wave optics will alter collective forms of consciousness. If consciousness itself arises from, or has its ground in, the embodied perceptions of the visible world, then the vision machines which saturate modern societies will come to shape the manner in which we are conscious of the world in new and unforeseen ways.

Some examples of contemporary communications media might be of help here. Satellite linkages and live feeds are now an eminently common feature of news broadcasting. With a live news report from another part of the globe we take for granted that something happening at the present moment is quasi-instantaneously transmitted to us. The analysis of the television image given earlier argued that the sense of proximity we may have while viewing such images is entirely illusory. It might be argued in this context that the more one lives on a day-to-day basis with the images of television the more they are taken for granted as a means of accessing the 'reality' of the world and the more their difference from immediate embodied perception is forgotten or obscured. In the case of live news footage the viewer is given an intense impression of immediacy or presence: we see a reporter *in situ* and are given a feeling of being close to the unfolding of events elsewhere. Yet this sense of immediacy, proximity and presence necessarily obscures all the complex material, cultural and commercial processes which inform the gathering and processing of information that govern modern journalism. On a day-to-day basis we access satellite and television media for instant news or live updates in order to get a sense of things 'as they happen' or of events 'as they unfold'. Doubtless we may be more or less sensitive to media bias in this area and to the notion of slanted coverage. The proliferation of satellite news media which represent different constituencies bears this out quite clearly: CNN and Fox News, despite their global reach, arguably report from a broadly specific American perspective or world view; Al Jazeera is directed towards a predominantly Arab, Middle

Eastern audience and, more recently, Latin American and French satellite news channels have been set up to counter the dominance of CNN and Fox News by offering a specifically Latin and French perspectives on events. This suggests that, awareness of bias or slanted coverage notwithstanding, we expect news coverage to offer a view of the world which more or less fits with our everyday perceptions of the way the world is or the way we think it should be. Television or satellite news, as it enters our living rooms, is another way of viewing the outside, another window on the world, as Virilio would put it, one whose transparency may slant our sight this way or that, but which nevertheless offers a possibility of seeing. Virilio argues that the images of television offer this sense of immediacy and presence because they are parasitic upon the everyday presence we experience as we orientate our bodies in the world. Television, he suggests, 'is parasitic upon the clear perception of the here and now' (Virilio 2000d: 4). He even goes on to assert that this parasitic nature of the televisual image as given to us in live transmission and satellite feeds comes to have a dominant role in the way we think about our wider shared experience in the world. Virilio describes a 'present telereality in "real time" which supplants the reality of the real presence of objects and places, with the passage of electromagnetic waves having the advantage' (Virilio 2000d: 6–7).

The notion of 'real time' comes to play a crucial role in his account of virtualization and telepresence. Scott McQuire in his work *Visions of Modernity* cites the coverage given to the release from prison of Nelson Mandela in 1991 as an example of the specific temporality which governs the images of live news footage. Echoing Virilio, McQuire suggests that live coverage, and television more generally, have their own temporal rhythm which privileges the instant of transmission over all else. The experience of this rhythm, he suggests, has become second nature to our viewing expectations (McQuire 1998: 255–6). When Mandela was released all the major news networks ran coverage in an attempt to show his emergence as a free man live and 'as it happened'. The release was delayed, however, leaving the cameras running in 'dead time'; broadcasters were left waiting with nothing happening, desperately trying to fill the moments of space, until many gave up and moved on with their pressing schedules. What this example shows is the manner in which the 'real time' of live footage is, like the 'light-time' or 'time of exposure' that Virilio talks about elsewhere, a temporality so focused on the intensity or presence of the instant that it elides the richness of lived temporality, with its retentions of past sensations and its purposeful yet uncertain anticipations of future possibility. It is a temporality in which, more often than not, there is an expectation that the event will be calculated in advance so that it can be packaged and sold to the viewer according to the commercial structures which underpin the whole business of news coverage. If, as was the case with Mandela in 1991, the event does not unfold as calculated, the entire time of transmission is wasted.

What the example of live television and news coverage suggests more generally, then, is the manner in which wave optics and its vision machines have come to alter the manner in which we view, relate to or understand the existence of the wider world. Parasitic on immediate presence, Virilio would argue that the telepresent images of television have indiscernibly come to substitute, in specific but decisive ways, for a lived and embodied engagement with the world. The temporality of 'real time' has become a dominant mode by which we experience world events as they are viewed or made virtually present in our living rooms. Virilio goes as far as to suggest that 'real time' and virtual presence have become the dominant mode of experience in those advanced societies which find themselves saturated with vision machines of all kinds. In *The Vision Machine* he speaks of the 'image in real time which dominates the thing represented, this time which henceforth overwhelms real space. This virtuality which dominates actuality, overturning the very notion of reality' (Virilio 1994b: 63). The question posed here is whether we have not become so used to mediated representations of the world that we have indiscernibly come to the point where telepresent representations have greater importance for us than lived embodied realities.

If one accepts that technological innovation is moving at such a pace that we have yet to develop concepts which might allow us fully to understand its impact, then Virilio's account of vision machines offers a means of critically approaching a whole range of questions relating to the contemporary life of advanced industrial or post-industrial societies. At the beginning of the twenty-first century there is, for instance, much talk in liberal democracies of the 'politics of spin' and much concern that the processes of the democratic polity have been undermined by the media and the need for politicians to present themselves in relation to the news media. The reality of public politics and therefore of government itself seems, to an ever greater extent, to be defined by the concerns of presentation. This leads one to question how much the force of the tele-image has come to overwhelm the real in the manner that Virilio suggests, or just how much disconnect there might be between our media image of the working of politics and government and what may really be going on. Alternatively, one might cite the invasion and subsequent occupation of Iraq in 2003. During the period in which this study was written American and British troops continued to occupy Iraq and there was intense debate as to the 'reality' of the situation there. For many of those who followed the course of this occupation there was an intense sense of disjunction between what was relayed in different ways through the broadcast media and a sense that the reality on the ground might be wholly other than the official versions of reality given.

It became clear, of course, that the optimistic official assessments of the British and American governments were deeply flawed as Iraq descended into ever greater sectarian conflict throughout 2006. Yet even as it became clear that the 'reality' in Iraq was far worse than governments had been willing to admit, the media presentation of reality did not cease to be highly politicized, disputed or manipulated according to the interests of different groupings. Journalists, of course, would insist that it is their job to seek and present the truth in the face of government spin and propaganda. Indeed, the very politicization of this issue and the varying representations of reality which are given suggest the extent to which we collectively rely on media representation to give us 'reality' in the first instance. At the same time we perhaps have an ambivalent feeling about the real status of the news and information we receive, whatever the source. It is as if the differing modes of perception that Virilio invokes, the viewing of telepresent images, and the seeing of lived experience, are in conflict with each other. We might put our faith in the former and assume we receive some measure of reality from telepresent images (and Virilio suggests that we unthinkingly do this all the time), or we might maintain a faith in the latter and accept, that, in the case of Iraq, we can know little about what is 'really going on'. Both these examples suggest that Virilio's account of vision machines and of virtual presence has important implications for the way in which we might approach or understand the nature of contemporary political life. This will be examined in more detail in the following chapter devoted to his account of war and politics.

Yet the dominance of telepresent reality and real time may be seen to have an impact on fundamental aspects of cultural life also. The question arises as to how far we may consciously or unconsciously come to privilege certain images of lived everyday experience over the living of that experience itself. The way in which television has become a collective mode of self-representation of individuals or communities raises this question in a particularly acute manner. When we watch reality television shows or talent competitions which involve 'normal' people with whom we can identify we are arguably participating in a form of mass self-identification. We approve or disapprove of particular identifiable types of individual with whom we can, to a greater or lesser extent, identify. We root for or support one contestant rather than another, depending on the mode of our identification. At the same time we knowingly participate in a synchronized event involving literally millions of people. If this is 'normal life' become spectacle then Virilio's contention that a certain kind of generalized tele-spectacle or tele-image has assumed a dominant role in relation to the lived real of life itself may be seen as a very pressing and urgent concern. The proliferation of film or recording technologies controlled by individuals may also offer an important example in this context. What is at stake when, for example, a tourist takes video footage of a tourist site such as the British Houses of Parliament, or when the immediate aftermath of a terrorist bombing is filmed on a mobile telephone by a victim of that very bombing? On one level the answer to both these questions may be quite simple: we like to have video footage to remember our holiday by. A victim of an attack will immediately be aware of the commercial worth of footage taken at the site of, and in seconds after, a terrorist attack. Both these answers are no doubt valid. Yet in both cases the importance of taking such film is arguably tied also to a shared sense that an event or act of perception is more properly lived or concretely experienced when recorded in the real time of video/mobile footage and then viewable by others in 'real time' at some other date. What is important in both cases is the value placed upon vision mediated by, and recorded with, a vision machine, whose original manufacture or eventual output is inserted into industrial processes and/or commercial interests. In *The Vision Machine* Virilio talks of a 'new industrialization of vision, the putting into place of a veritable market of synthetic perception' (Virilio 1994b: 59). The various examples cited here – of live news footage and the media presentation of politics, of reality television and digital recording of personal experience – may, of course, be interpreted in any number of ways. No doubt sociological or political science discourses could all shed light on various aspects of these phenomena. What all these examples demonstrate, however, albeit in a preliminary and provisional manner, is that Virilio's thinking about virtual presence can offer a powerful critical and speculative tool for engaging with fundamental structures of perception as they are mediated by technology. This, in turn, allows us to understand aspects of contemporary reality in new and productive ways.

This chapter began by highlighting the rather apocalyptic or excessively pessimistic tone of some of Virilio's pronouncements about the impact of speed machines in the modern world. What this discussion has sought to emphasize is that the account of speed machines, vision machines and virtual presence given in his writing as a whole is of interest because of the way in which it allows a different kind of analysis to occur. If Virilio's writing can at times appear apocalyptic or over-pessimistic, it is because his analysis is deeply rooted in a certain strand of phenomenological thought which retains a profound attachment to, and affirmation of, the notion of the situated body and of the material spatiality of lived, embodied experience. Readers of Virilio's texts should decide for themselves the extent to which his more pessimistic judgements reflect the reality of our collective involvement with contemporary technologies of speed. Yet, if this phenomenological approach leads Virilio to make sweepingly negative statements in relation to modern technology, it also allows a thinking which places fundamental structures of perception, experience and spatial–temporal orientation at the centre of its critical concerns. This allows questions to be asked in ways which might otherwise not be possible. Virilio's is a discourse which allows us to ask, in a rigorous and grounded theoretical manner, about the way in which our perceptions of time, space and presence are being altered. His writing allows us to address the manner which this transformation of perception has an impact in all areas of life: from the personal to the public, the military to the political, from the urban and architectural sphere through to the broader sphere of cultural life more generally. What if, for instance, we are coming to experience the present in a subtly different way, will that have an effect on the way we retain the past and remember our shared history? Will tendencies in the present that we cannot identify quite clearly come to dominate our experience more and more in the future? Above all is our preoccupation with the time and virtual images of instantaneous transmission slowly attenuating or eroding our relation to the real space and geographical extension of the world (and this at a time of unprecedented danger for the well-being of the physical global environment)? Rather than a doom-laden prediction of apocalypse Virilio's texts might best be read as a critical 'what if?' Towards the end of *The Vision Machine* he writes: 'if real time is coming to overwhelm real space, if the image is overwhelming the object, or, indeed, being-present itself, if the virtual is coming to overwhelm actuality, then it is necessary to analyse the consequences of this "intensive time" on different physical representations"' (Virilio 1994b: 73).

The key terms developed by Virilio to address the becoming virtual of experience, namely the aesthetics of disappearance, telepresence, vision and speed machines, real time, light-time or an intensive time of exposure, all these terms should be viewed as analytical-critical tools developed from within a specific phenomenological perspective. If the speed of technological progress can appear at times bewildering or intensely disorientating then such tools may prove to be indispensable for any understanding of present and future technological development. The remainder of this study will examine further Virilio's thinking about perception, speed and virtualization in three specific areas: war, politics and the development of modern and contemporary art and cinema.

SUMMARY

Virilio's account of the virtualization of experience in modern media is often couched in apocalyptic or catastrophist terms. He contends that technologies of speed precipitate a decline of lived spatial existence and a crisis in our collective representations of the world. Despite this dominant note of pessimism his writing about virtual presence does allow us to engage critically with nature of cinematic, televisual and other media images or forms of communication. Virilio's focus on the phenomenology of perception allows him to highlight the manner in which the images of cinema and television are 'telepresent', that is to say, present at a distance or in their absence. Telepresence, according to Virilio's account, brings with it a privileging of the instant of transmission at the expense of an experience of material or spatial extension. The 'real time' of telepresence is one in which the being of sensible forms is altered: the virtual comes to dominate over the actual, the exposure of the calculated instant dominates over the richness and diversity of embodied temporality or duration. Virilio suggests that modern vision machines have invented an entirely new way of seeing, that is, vision as mediated through the transmission of radio waves or electronic pulses, and that this 'wave optics' has the potential to transform the manner in which we are conscious of ourselves and of the world. The world of vision machines and wave optics is one in which diverse aspects of cultural and political life can be altered in fundamental ways.

4

WAR

Bunkers, pure war and
the fourth front

In an interview with Sylvère Lotringer published originally in 1983 Virilio indicates that his interest in war is inseparable from his interest in the city and urban planning. It is also, he emphasizes, an interest which has its roots in his personal history, namely the experience of the Second World War and, specifically, of the aerial bombardment and destruction of the city of Nantes which he witnessed when he was ten years old (Virilio and Lotringer 1997: 10). In this context Virilio identifies what he calls 'two great schools of thought on urban planning'. The first situates the origins of the city and urban sedentariness in mercantilism (that is trade, commerce, and its accompanying social formations). The second situates the origins of the city in war. Aligning himself squarely with the latter school of thought, Virilio nevertheless freely admits that this is a minority view shared by some prominent figures, but which is most often eclipsed by the majority school which locates the origin of urbanism in mercantilism (Virilio and Lotringer 1997: 11). This is a position adopted by Virilio consistently throughout his career, one which underpins nearly everything he has to say about war and technology or the relation between war and politics. As he puts it in his book about the first Gulf War, *Desert Screen*: 'To say that the City and War go hand in glove is a euphemism. The city, the *polis*, is constitutive of the form of conflict called WAR, just as war is itself constitutive of the political form called the CITY' (Virilio 2005e: 4).

By situating the origin of the city in war, Virilio also affirms the insep-arability of war from politics. Politics, defined as the art of governing the internal and external affairs of a specific entity (e.g. a state), is a word derived from the term *polis*, the Ancient Greek city-state (e.g. Athens or Sparta). These Ancient Greek states were urban formations but also distinct political entities which would most likely have controlled surrounding countryside or hinterland. The emphasis Virilio places on war as the origin of the city, and therefore on war as a fundamental factor in the shaping or formation of political life, necessarily places economics in a secondary position. This runs against the grain of much modern orthodoxy, which, in the wake of thinkers such as Adam Smith, would situate economics as a primary or fundamental sphere of human activity. A thinker like Smith believed that the propensity to barter, trade and exchange goods is a common and universal feature which, in an essential way, distinguishes man from animals (thus man is fundamentally *homo oeconomicus*) (Smith 1993: 21). From his earliest works Virilio rejects this position outright. In *Speed and Politics*, for instance, he writes of modern liberal (or what he terms 'bourgeois') political structures: 'Bourgeois power is military even more than economic, but it relates most directly to the occult permanence of the state of siege, to the appearance of fortified towns' (Virilio 1986: 11). Politics and political forms have, according to Virilio, their roots in the space of the city such as it is shaped by the forces of war.

In this context economics as we know it, that is to say, the everyday life of economic activity which governs the flow of commodities, wealth and goods during peacetime, is a secondary phenomenon which takes its shape from the war economy and the material and logistical necessities which govern conflict during times of war. For Virilio war is first and foremost a matter of logistics, that is, the procurement, maintenance and distribution of weapons, material and personnel, as well as the overall management and strategy of armed conflict. He is primarily interested in the space of war, the movement of armies, weapons, material and information through that space, and the manner in which military space then comes to shape social and political space. In the interview with Sylvère Lotringer cited above the centrality he gives to the concept of military space is made very clear (Virilio and Lotringer 1997: 10). He also clearly affirms the primacy of military logistics in relation to economy: 'Logistics is the beginning of the economy of war, which will then become simple economy, to the point of replacing political economy' (Virilio and Lotringer 1997: 12). From this perspective, then, the organization of military space and of military logistics is a key determining factor in the formation not only of political space, but of economic life also.

The priority Virilio gives to the military sphere leads him to make some characteristically sweeping claims, as, for instance, in *Popular Defence and Ecological Struggles*: 'It was not only the disciplining of intelligence and of bodies, or the elimination of individual patterns of behaviour which was developed on the battlefields of civil or foreign wars, but rather the ethics of the entire industrial world' (Virilio 1990: 29). By this account war not only shapes political and economic activity (e.g. the emergence of fortified towns and their accompanying political formations), it has a profound impact on the very nature of society's shared outlook, its values and its ideals. For Virilio, then: 'War . . . is the fundamental concept of our civilization' (Virilio 1990: 22), or more specifically, war 'forms the constitutional base of the great modern States' (Virilio 1990: 46). Taken in isolation such claims will inevitably have the character of sweeping historical generalization rather than sober analytical assessments. Yet, as always with Virilio's writing, more general claims like these can be understood only in relation to the broader detail of the arguments he puts forth. What follows in this chapter will evaluate the specifics of some of Virilio's arguments in relation to war and will examine in particular his analysis of the development of weapons and communications from the First World War through to the first Gulf War. It will also highlight the manner in which his thinking diverges from that of one of the best known theorists of war, Carl von Clausewitz, whose famous dictum, 'War is the continuation of politics by other means,' is referred to by Virilio, directly or indirectly, on a number of occasions (e.g. Virilio and Lotringer 1997: 31; Virilio 2000c: 49; Armitage 2001: 95; see also Clausewitz 1968: 119, 402). Where Clausewitz clearly separates politics from war and places the former in a primary position in relation to the latter (since war is a continuation of political activity) (Clausewitz 1968: 119, 402), Virilio appears to invert this relation. Politics may here be said to be the continuation of war by other means. However, it might be more accurate to suggest, that, for Virilio, war plays such a fundamental role in shaping the space of the political that the two spheres no longer maintain any clear or distinct identity such that one might be said to be the continuation of the other.

This blurring of the distinction between war and politics is of particular significance for the account Virilio gives of twentieth-century conflicts. As will become clear, in the context of the Cold War and the logic of nuclear deterrence the very distinction between war and peace itself is also called into question. The fundamental role played by military space in the structuring of the political and social spheres is the dominant preoccupation of Virilio's first full-length work, *Bunker Archeology*, published in the original French in 1975. This first work takes as its subject matter the concrete blockhouses of the Atlantic seaboard which were erected by Nazi Germany in the early 1940s. The book itself is made up of a number of short medi-tations and a collection of surprisingly beautiful photographs of the blockhouses themselves. Virilio's fascination with the remnants of Nazi fortifications may at first seem rather idiosyncratic. The argument of *Bunker Archeology*, however, suggests that it is in the existence of such fortifications that we can discern the complex and perhaps hidden interrelation of war, politics and the shaping of urban and geopolitical space.

BUNKER ARCHEOLOGY

In order to understand the key significance accorded to concrete fortifications in *Bunker Archeology* it is necessary to understand the broader speculative history which underpins Virilio's account of warfare in general. A brief outline of such a speculative history is given at the beginning of *Popular Defence and Ecological Struggles*, published originally in 1978 three years after the appearance of *Bunker Archeology*. Here Virilio suggests that in its origin violent conflict was a more or less spontaneous enterprise, conducted without any specific strategy, war scenario or theatre planned in advance:

> The act of violence formed a real part of the set of still badly defined social exchanges . . . [men] did not use obstacles or artificial fortifi-cations and knew perfectly how to use their environment in order to camouflage themselves, move from place to place or hide but *not in order to defend themselves*.

> (Virilio 1990: 13–14)

The development and history of warfare are, by this account, very much a matter of different ways of organizing the space of conflict and, in particular, the different ways in which conflict involves movement through the environment coupled with specific means of attack and defence. The suggestion here is that early populations of human beings who may have lived as hunter gatherers would have entered into conflict in a more or less unplanned fashion as different groupings competed for natural resources in the environment.

The question of war properly speaking arises only with the ambition to control the space and procedures of conflict in a more sustained manner. In this context Virilio hypothesizes that the strategic and military planning which characterize war are likely to have emerged as a reaction against the more or less unformed and spontaneous nature of early conflict (Virilio 1990: 14). The construction of fortifications, ramparts and other defensive structures becomes necessary only when the space of the environment is conceived in advance as a theatre for possible military engagements and when the military possibilities offered by this space have been thought out beforehand. Virilio puts this in the following terms:

If the Ancients appeared at first as constructors of ramparts and fortifications, this was because the ambition to wage [*conduire*] war begins
with the project of the war theatre, that is to say the creation of *artificial
environmental conditions* which will form the infrastructure, the scene
where the movement of the war scenario will have to unfold according
to the advance preparations of the adversary who plans to dominate
the other.

(Virilio 1990: 14–15)

If war is conceived as primarily a matter of an artificial construction and strategic use of the space of the environment then the fundamental role played by military planning in the shaping of social and political space becomes clear. The need to concentrate human habitation in strategically defensible areas or to surround that habitation with fortifications arises only within the context of the projection and planning of specific possibilities of military conflict. This military projection of space is organized around the potential for movements of attack and the manner in which the use of terrain (e.g. hilltop settlements) or fortifications (e.g. surrounding walls) can work to block such enemy movement and prevent its penetration into settlement space. Once the more or less spontaneous manoeuvres of engagement or flight have been abandoned (with the development of more settled agrarian populations) the aim of the military planner is 'to attempt to retain *on one's own ground the advantage* over the enemy, and from this arises the construction of protected enclaves, surrounding walls and palisades around the hilltop settlement all destined to slow down the aggressor' (Virilio 1990: 15). From the point of view of the aggressor it becomes necessary to develop techniques of assault or penetration which will overcome the defensive capacities offered by hilltop settlement and fortifications. War, then, emerges as such only in the context of very specific and strategic thinking about the environment and the possibilities of attack and defence which arise within that context.

This may seem like stating nothing other than the obvious. Yet, as always with Virilio's analyses, it is essential to highlight the importance he places on spatial orientation, movement and the relative speeds of movement that specific forms of spatial organization permit. In this context Virilio often cites the Ancient Chinese theorist of war, Sun Tzu, who once wrote that 'Speed is the essence of war' (e.g. Virilio 1986: 133; Armitage 2001: 75; Virilio 2005a: 102; see also Sun Tzu 1963: 134). By this account the essence of war lies in the relative speeds of attack and defence, the former being a principle of acceleration or possibility of movement, the latter being a principle of inertia or the attempt to block movement. Virilio expresses it in the following terms: 'Attack and defence divide on the terrain of battle to form two elements of the same dialectic: the first becoming synonymous with speed, circulation, progression and change, the second as opposition to movement' (Virilio 1990: 15–16). Such fundamental insights into the origins and essence of war underpin both the account Virilio gives of its general historical development and the particular arguments he puts forward in relation to the specific instances of war he discusses.

This is true of his meditation on the significance of the Second World War bunkers of the Atlantic seaboard in *Bunker Archeology*. At key points in this, his first full-length work, Virilio alludes to the fundamental importance of military planning in the shaping of social space and to the manner in which the organization of territorial space and relative speeds of movement and penetration are interlinked:

The necessity of *controlling* constantly expanding territory, of scanning it in all directions . . . while running up against as few obstacles as possible has constantly justified the increase in the penetration speed of means of transport and communications . . . as well as the speed of the arsenal's projectiles.

(Virilio 1994a: 17)

There is thus a hierarchy of speeds to be found in the history of societies, for to possess the earth, to hold terrain, is also to possess the best means to scan it in order to protect and defend it.

(Virilio 1994a: 19)

Comments such as these demonstrate the way in which the 'dromological' perspective lies at the centre of Virilio's concerns from his earliest published work. They recall the notion of speed-space discussed in Chapter 2, that is to say, space as defined by relative movements and by the relative or changing speed of those movements. In this case it is less a matter of bodily orientation and embodied perception and more a matter of the planning and organization of environmental space according to the needs and possibilities of military planning. This fundamental interconnection of military space and speed-space and the primary role played by them in the formation of political space (i.e. that of the *polis* or city) have as a consequence a more general blurring of the distinction between war and peace. As will become clear this blurring is one of the key features of Virilio's analysis of war in general and of twentieth-century conflict in particular. In *Bunker Archeology* he expresses this by highlighting once more the key role played by fortifications:

> The fortification answers to the accidental, the duel between arms and armour leaves its mark on the organization of territory by progress in its means and methods, by the potentialities of its inventions – war is thus present in peacetime. A history unravels itself parallel to the history of civilian production; powers and energies develop ceaselessly in the constantly renewed perspective of conflict, but this production, secret and surprising, is ignored.
>
> (Virilio 1994a: 43)

The account Virilio gives of the existence of concrete bunkers in *Bunker Archeology* is, precisely, an archaeology, that is to say, an attempt to uncover a hidden aspect of the past through an encounter with its material remains. In order to understand the manner in which war is present in peacetime, or, more precisely, the manner in which the boundary which separates war and peace is in reality always permeable, Virilio highlights the key role played by the concrete bunkers, both in the military and the political imagination of Nazi Germany and in the more general history of warfare and fortification.

In this context concrete fortifications appear not just as defensive structures designed for the repulsion of a specific military threat (in this case the possible invasion by sea of Allied forces towards the end of the Second World War). They also act as indicators of the manner in which military, and therefore political, space has been conceived. In fact Virilio sees these concrete structures as monuments of the inner logic of the Third Reich; they testify to a certain mode of ideological organization proper to the Nazi regime and to a specific logic which led, perhaps inexorably, to its destruction. In this context he affirms, somewhat elliptically, that 'the bunkers of the European littoral were from the start the funerary monuments to the German dream' (Virilio 1994a: 29). First and foremost these bunkers testify to the manner in which so much of Nazi political thinking and military planning was orientated around specific conceptions of space and the appropriation of living space for the German peoples. The bunkers or casemates (i.e. fortified enclosures) mark the natural outer limit of a certain territorial organization or aspiration in Western Europe and form a specific component part of that mode of organization. In this context Virilio alludes to the term 'Fortress Europe', that is, the aspiration of the Nazi high command to create in the space of the European continent a more or less homogenized entity whose borders and inner organization would be subject to the control of military power. The existence of the concrete bunkers would be unthinkable, Virilio argues, without the prior projection of the space of Europe as a military space, a fortress conceived according to the aspirations of Nazi ideology: 'The Fortress Europe was three-dimensional, the casemates on the beaches complemented the aircraft shelters of the cities. . . . Space was at last homogenized, absolute war had become a reality, and the monolith was its monument' (Virilio 1994a: 40). Here the concrete bunkers far exceed their practical use as defensive structures used in the protection of a specific locus or terrain. As monoliths they take on a monumental or symbolic quality. They represent a certain aspiration to master or totalize the space of a continent. Virilio remarks on the sheer scale of a project which sought to militarize such a great length of the European seaboard: 'The immensity of the project is what defies common sense; total war was revealed here in its mythic dimension' (Virilio 1994a: 12).

It is within the context of this mythic dimension that the concrete bunkers can be seen as 'the funerary monuments to the German dream'. As fortifications they testify to the military organization of the Third Reich and therefore are deeply implicated in its political and ideological organization. Yet they also exist within a long history of warfare which, according to Virilio's account, develops according to a dialectic of attack and defence and the relative speeds (of acceleration or inertia) proper to both. In this context the defensive character of the bunkers evidently lies in a principle of inertia, that is to say, they will block the forward movement of the enemy. As such their function is tied narrowly to the space of terrain or territorial ambition. They have little defensive power in relation to the speeds of penetration accomplished by aircraft. Virilio remarks at some length on the manner in which the greater part of German strategy was focused on territorial ambition and the control of land at the expense of aerial or naval strategy (Virilio 1994a: 29). It is this fixation with territory, with living space and with the militarization of frontiers according to the logic of Fortress Europe which confers upon the bunkers their strategic defensive importance, their mythic and symbolic importance, but also their significance as a key moment in the history of warfare and in the construction of military and political space.

For Virilio the Second World War represents a decisive transition in the history of military planning and the dialectic of attack and defence which underpins it. This is because of the systematic introduction of aerial bombardment and the targeting of civilian populations and industrial or urban sites. This opening up in a more general way of a third front (after those of the land and the sea) radically transforms military strategy and in so doing transforms the nature of military space. If the aim is no longer to win a war purely by capturing territory, but to win the war by destroying urban and industrial infrastructure through aerial bombardment, then fortifications whose function is to block movement across land cease to have any primary value. Aerial bombardment itself dates back to the First World War. The Third Reich pioneered the technique of bombing urban centres, first during the Spanish Civil War with the destruction of Guernica, and then early in the Second World War with the Blitzkrieg offensive over London. Later in the war the bombing and destruction of a wide range of cities becomes a central or systematic plank of the military strategy adopted by the Allies. The impact of such a strategy upon the defensive value of concrete bunkers is highlighted by Virilio as a decisive moment: 'the destruction of the great European cities completely broke down the shielding effect of littoral and frontier fortification' (Virilio 1994a: 47).

With frontiers no longer being the key line of defence that organizes strategic military thinking the very notion of the frontier as a political or geopolitical unit of value changes. As hundreds of miles of seaboard fortifications become far less important within the overall organization and projection of military space, the structure and organization of political and geopolitical space may itself begin to shift. This, at least is Virilio's contention, for he sees in the redundancy of concrete bunkers nothing less than an indicator of a huge geopolitical transformation. 'These concrete bunkers,' he asserts, 'were in fact the throw-offs of the history of frontiers'

(Virilio 1994a: 12). To encounter them in the post-war period, as Virilio himself did in the 1950s, is to encounter the material remains of a previous form of military and political organization. Virilio expresses this by once again underscoring the monumental or mythic dimension of these concrete fortifications: 'the concrete landmark indicates the place where the long organization of territorial infrastructures comes to an end, from the steps of the empire, to the borders of the state, to the continental threshold. The bunker has become a myth' (Virilio 1994a: 46). This is perhaps the central thesis or argument of *Bunker Archeology* as a whole. It is an argument which views the archaeological remains of these Atlantic coast blockhouses within the context of a broad historical vision and views them above all as indicators of a transitional moment in the military-political orientation of the modern world.

It could perhaps be remarked that Virilio is placing a disproportionate weight of significance on what was, after all, a collection of poured concrete blocks. Yet the real importance lies, of course, with the systematic opening up of the third front of the air as a means of waging total war, that is, a war which not only targets standing armies or military sites, but engages the entirety of the economy, and which targets also the entire civilian population, in particular the dense concentration of urban populations. The logic of total war can be seen to inform the outlook of both antagonists during the Second World War. It is at work in the Nazi aspirations to a Fortress Europe, a homogenized and militarized living space at the disposal of the German people, and it is, of course, clearly proclaimed in the rhetoric of *Totalkrieg* used by the regime during the height of the conflict (e.g. in Goebbels's appeal for the waging of total war in his speech and radio broadcast of February 1943). In the sense most explicitly invoked by Virilio the Second World War is a total war when, with the aerial bombing of the cities, the entire space of the civilian and urban environment becomes a potential target and when nowhere appears safe from the risk of military attack. This logic of totalization implicit in the systematic exploitation of the third front of air attack is of crucial importance for Virilio's analysis since it underpins both the significance he accords to the bunkers of the Atlantic littoral and to the new age of war which follows from their implicit redundancy after the advent of aerial bombing. The redundancy of these fortifications presages nothing less than the arrival of that most powerful of all weapons, the nuclear bomb. More than their defensive capacity and its imminent obsolescence, the blockhouses are symbolic of a turning point or a cusp of history. They mark a moment of transition from the territorial wars of states and empires to a new kind of war where the threat of total destruction is the primary means of waging battle. In Virilio's own words, 'The bunker is the proto-history of an age in which the power of a single weapon is so great that no distance can protect you from it any longer' (Virilio 1994a: 46).

TOTAL PEACE – PURE WAR

Perhaps one of the most startling conclusions that Virilio draws from his analysis in *Bunker Archeology*, one upon which he builds in subsequent works, is that the Second World War did not come to an end (Virilio 1994a: 58). The logic of total war is such that the state of war itself becomes limitless. Virilio draws this conclusion because he sees an essential continuity between the aerial bombing of European and Japanese cities and the threat of extermination posed to civilian populations by nuclear weapons in the post-war period. If the redundancy of frontier fortifications signals the advent of total war, then the advent of the nuclear bomb and the threat of extermination it implies inaugurates a period of what Virilio terms 'Total Peace'. This continuity between the total war of aerial bombardment and the total peace of nuclear deterrence, and by implication the absence of any real distinction between war and peace in the post-war period, could be defended with simple reference to the actual use of nuclear weapons in Hiroshima and Nagasaki. The deployment of nuclear payloads was arguably a direct extension of the strategy of bombing urban centres which was already in place and, whilst the destruction of the two Japanese cities clearly brought hostilities between the Allied and Axis powers to a close, it was also the opening chapter of what came to be called the Cold War, that is, the nuclear stand-off between the United States and the Soviet Union. For Virilio the Total Peace of nuclear deterrence is an inverted continuation of the total war of aerial bombardment, or as he puts it in an interview with Sylvère Lotringer, 'the Second World War never ended . . . There's no state of peace. It isn't over because it continued in Total Peace, that is, in war pursued by other means' (Virilio and Lotringer 1997: 30–1). Here Virilio inverts Clausewitz's statement about war being a continuation of politic and transforms it into the following: 'the Total Peace of deterrence is T' War pursued by other means' (Virilio and Lotringer 1997: 31).

Looked at from this perspective the claim that the Second Wo did not come to an end is perhaps not so startling, although it cle' the question of what a 'cold war' might be in different terms. T' is taken up by Virilio in the work published immediately after *Bunker Archeology* in 1976, entitled *The Insecurity of Territory* (*L'Insécurité du territoire*). Once again he emphasizes the manner in which the Second World War can be seen as a transitional moment of decisive importance in the history of conflict and the political structures which are shaped by military space. Here he focuses again on the impact of aerial warfare: 'Total war was a threshold for our civilization to the extent that it was the first global aerial war' (Virilio 1993: 92). The shift from total war to total peace needs to be understood quite specifically in the context of the technology of war, and the dialectic of attack and defence which, according to Virilio, provides the motor for the development of war technology. Here he suggests that the transition from total war to total peace is an implicit necessity of technological progress which will inevitably aim to increase the power, speed and penetration of weaponry: 'Already, total war carried within it its technical self-surpassing, the Cold War then total peace' (Virilio 1993: 133). Yet, however much aerial bombing and nuclear deterrence might seem very different from each other, Virilio argues that they bring about in reality the same state of affairs, that is, a generalized insecurity of civilian populations on the basis of which military strategy is pursued: 'the principle of these successive strategies derives only from the creation and expansion of civil insecurity inside national frontiers, an insecurity which would have been inconceivable a few decades earlier' (Virilio 1993: 133). The assertion that the Second World War did not come to an end is not simply an abstract redrawing of the distinction between war and peace. For Virilio the continuation of total war in the shape of total peace implies a very real lived insecurity on the part of civilian populations (as those who lived through this period may all readily testify). As was shown earlier, Virilio questions in more general terms the distinction between war and peace, since he affirms the presence of war in peacetime (Virilio 1994a: 43) and the 'occult permanence of the state of siege' (Virilio 1986: 11). Yet the Second World War marks a point where this more general permeability of the two states is radicalized to the point where even the experience of a state of war and a state of peace becomes more radically indistinct. For Virilio the logic of nuclear deterrence brings with it nothing less than the end of the distinction between these two states and signifies 'the end of the centuries-old alternative between war and peace, the passage of total war to a new and unknown state: total peace'. If, hitherto, war was present in peacetime, or subsisted into peacetime in an 'occult state of siege', henceforth the two states fold into each other to form an entirely new military and political form.

This state of total peace is closely connected to what, in subsequent works, Virilio comes to call 'pure war'. Both these terms are used in relation to the logic of nuclear deterrence, but it is arguable that 'pure war' becomes a far more all-embracing theoretical term in so far as it more directly implies, not just a military strategy based on generalized insecurity, but comes to stand as a figure for a global, technological, economic and even metaphysical organization the state and of collective experience. Pure war is similar to total peace in so far as both imply the conflation of the states of war and peace described above. In *Popular defence and Ecological Struggles* Virilio expresses this as follows: 'PURE WAR is neither peace nor war, nor is, as we may have believed, "absolute" or "total" war, rather it is the military instance in its perennial ordinariness' (Virilio 1990: 35). Yet, arguably, the term 'pure war', in Virilio, develops further some of the assumptions which were already implicit in 'total peace'. In *The Insecurity of Territory* nuclear deterrence is described as a strategy which strips warfare of its contingent aspects: 'the bomb does not suppress war, it suppresses a certain number of its random elements [hazards] while shifting strategic decision making into other categories' (Virilio 1993: 143). The bomb, as it were, 'purifies' war of the random or accidental possibilities of the battlefield and places decision making with those who plan strategy, make decisions to site missile silos or, indeed, press the nuclear trigger. More generally Virilio refers to the doctrine of nuclear deterrence as a: 'conspiracy, in which science and technology radiate their all-powerfulness, and become mystical figures' (Virilio 1993: 140). It is these two aspects, that is, the stripping from war of the contingency of the battlefield, and the raising of technological power to the level of a mystical or metaphysical figure, which come to characterize Virilio's use of the term 'pure war'. War in its 'pure' form appears almost to transcend the question of conflict *per se* and to become a mode of organizing or structuring the whole of human reality. It is located in the scientific or techno-scientific view of the world, that is, 'war operating in the sciences . . . everything that is perverting the field of knowledge' (Virilio and Lotringer 1997: 27). Unlike total peace, pure war is to be seen less in relation to a specific conflict (e.g. the Second World War) and far more in terms of techno-scientific discovery. Pure war, for Virilio, isn't 'tied down to confrontation between East and West, but to the development of science as techno-science' (Virilio and Lotringer 1997: 167). In the final analysis, it appears to describe an almost religious attitude rather than a specific mode of conflict: 'Pure War is the absolute idol . . . Pure War is entirely comparable to that of the idol in ancient societies' (Virilio and Lotringer 1997: 164). It is an 'ultimate metaphysical figure' (Virilio 1990: 102).

What these citations imply is a development in Virilio's thinking during the 1970s. His meditation on the concrete fortifications of the Atlantic seaboard is inserted into a wider thinking about the technology of war. The archaeological remains of the bunkers become a key symbol of a transformation of military and political space brought about by the opening up of the third front of aerial bombardment. From this Virilio concludes that the Cold War period following the Second World War was, in fact, a period of total peace, that is to say, the continuation of war by other means (nuclear deterrence). This, in turn, develops into a thinking of pure war, a thinking which more explicitly foregrounds the techno-scientific ideology which underpins nuclear deterrence as both a mode of organizing the whole of human society and a metaphysical figure or belief system which shapes a collective view of reality. In effect Virilio moves from a thinking of military technologies which shape social and political space to a thinking of a military-technological world view which shapes our entire apprehension of reality. Pure war becomes, for Virilio, a modern cult, a 'military-scientific messianism' which underpins the global order of security based on nuclear weapons.

It might be argued that Virilio's account of pure war is too all-embracing, too much inflected by his Christian background, or what Steve Redhead calls his 'Catholic anti-statism' (Redhead 2004: 85). In his privileging of the body proper of phenomenology (see Chapter 1) or of an implicitly Christian conception of the human (both of which would place the techno-logical in a secondary position) Virilio could be said to be more than a little technophobic and therefore overemphasize the structural and ideological importance of military and techno-scientific thinking. It has been suggested here, however, that his general account of war, and the more specific account of bunkers, total peace and pure war, are of value in so far as they allow us to interrogate the fundamental ways in which military, political, social and ideological space may be profoundly interlinked. If nuclear deterrence is to be understood not just as a military strategy or doctrine, but also as an ideology which is inseparable from a broader technological and political worldview or belief system, then Virilio's analysis serves to deepen or at the very least stimulate our understanding.

As always with his arguments what is of primary importance is the constitution of space, the relative rates of movement or penetration through what can, as elsewhere in Virilio's writing, be called 'speed-space'.

Ultimately what is at stake is the manner in which (military) technology and speed-space interact to create possibilities of spatial organization which then form some basic elements of collective experience and consciousness (i.e. social and political life). For Virilio the advent of aerial bombs, ballistic missiles and nuclear payloads or warheads poses questions which are fundamental and cannot be ignored. Yet if the technologies of the third front of the aerial warfare are decisive for this account, the advent of what Virilio calls the 'fourth front' is of no less importance.

LOGISTICS OF PERCEPTION AND THE FOURTH FRONT

It was suggested earlier in this discussion that the 'speed-space' of warfare, as thought by Virilio, was less orientated around questions of embodied perception and far more concerned with the relative speeds of acceleration and inertia (corresponding to the modes of attack and defence respectively). Yet this is true only in relation to the account he gives of the material logistics of warfare, concerned as it is with assault, weaponry and fortification. From *Bunker Archeology* onwards, in fact, he clearly emphasizes that the military projection and planning which make war possible is also fundamentally a matter of perception and representation:

> Anticipation and ubiquity are war's requirement and distance or prominent obstacles must not impede intelligence or reconnaissance. On the one hand one must see all and hear all and know all, and, on the other, one must create masks and screens infinitely tighter than any nature offered.
> (Virilio 1994a: 43)

This is not so much about embodied perception as it is about what Virilio comes to call 'logistics of perception'. If war is, in its essence, a matter of relative speed through space, this is nevertheless inseparable from the perception of space. It could be said that the movement of attack corresponds to the need to 'see all and hear all and know all' on the one hand, and that the movement of defence corresponds to the creation of 'masks and screens' on the other. A battle, then, is as much about being able to see and aim correctly in order to destroy the enemy as it is about having the weapons to do so. It is as much about manipulating what the enemy can see through ruses or modes of camouflage as it is about having impregnable defences or fortification. To this extent 'every conflict', for Virilio, 'is a field of perception. The field of battle is first of all a field of perception' (Virilio 1999: 26). This question of perception and specifically the notion of a 'logistics of perception' forms the second principal strand of Virilio's thinking about war.

This argument is developed at length in *War and Cinema I* which was published originally in 1984 and subtitled *Logistics of perception*. The last chapter argued that Virilio's arguments regarding the 'becoming virtual' of experience relied very heavily on an account of the role played by the rise of cinema in the late nineteenth and early twentieth centuries. In particular it argued that, for Virilio, the 'aesthetics of disappearance' of the cinematic image was a forerunner of the virtual presence of television, satellite and digital media. A similar development can be traced whereby the cinema is shown to have had a decisive impact on the waging of war between 1914 and 1918 in a way which prefigures the role played by broadcast media in contemporary warfare. In *War and Cinema I* Virilio repeats his basic premise regarding warfare and perception, namely that 'There is no war without representation' (Virilio 1989: 6) and that 'the battlefield has always been a field of perception' (Virilio 1989: 20). He then builds on this premise, arguing that the use of photography for aerial reconnaissance and of cinema footage for news and propaganda purposes was a key moment in changing the nature of warfare between 1914 and 1918. The increasing use of photographic and cinematic technology on the battlefield was, according this account, made necessary by the changing nature of weaponry, that is to say, the introduction of distance shelling and rapid-fire artillery:

If the First World War is the first mediatized conflict in history this is because rapid-fire weapons supplant the multitude of individual weapons. It is the end of systematic arm-to-arm combat and physical confrontation and the beginning of carnage at a distance where the adversary is invisible or nearly, *with the exception of assault flares* which signal the necessity of optical aiming, telescopic enlargement, the importance of the *war film* and the photographic restitution of the battlefield, but also and above all observation aviation in the carrying out of operations.

(Virilio 1989: 69–70)

In this sense the two different logistics of warfare, that of weapons and materiel and that of perception and representation, appear to be fundamentally interlinked. As the possibility of attack within military space becomes determined by rapid bombardment at distances which outstrip the capacity of normal or direct viewing, so more indirect means of viewing become necessary. One only needs to compare the way in which a cannon might once have been aimed according to a direct line of sight to the aiming of shell rounds according to calculated trajectories and map co-ordinates to understand the significance of Virilio's insight here. The rise of photographic and cinematic technologies in the waging of war point to a 'conjunction between the power of the modern war machine, the plane and the new capabilities of observation machines: aerial photography, the cinemato-graphic photogram' (Virilio 1989: 71).

Once again Virilio detects in the development of photographic and cinematic technologies a shift from direct to indirect viewing. The act of aiming along a direct line of sight is substituted with an indirect seeing, or a seeing-at-a-distance whereby the enemy can be located and targeted through the medium of photographic paper or celluloid. This shift clearly repeats, in the military space of the battlefield, the transition from direct to indirect seeing which, according to Virilio, more generally characterizes the development of photography and cinema in the early twentieth century (as discussed in the previous chapter). At the same time this shift is seen to have fundamental implications for the nature of battle and warfare itself, implications which far exceed the process of locating and targeting enemy positions. The introduction of new visual means of perceiving and repre-senting the battlefield signifies, for Virilio, nothing less than the turning of war itself into a kind of spectacle.

In this context, the representation of battle can become a weapon or a means of dominating the enemy as much as any explosive shell or artillery round. The importance of these new visual technologies cannot be under-stood without reference to the symbolic dimension of war. Here war is not simply a matter of physical suppression or annihilation but a matter of dominating the enemy's spirit, morale and will to do battle. This is a dimension which, according to Virilio, has always been present in warfare:

> War cannot detach itself from magical spectacle because the production of this spectacle is its goal: destroying the enemy is less a matter of cap-turing him than it is a matter of captivating him; it is a matter of inflicting upon him, before his death, the horror of death.
>
> (Virilio 1989: 5)

With the development of the indirect viewing of photography and cinema this spectacular dimension of warfare takes on ever more dominant role.

Much of Virilio's analysis in *War and Cinema* traces in some considerable detail the development of cinema as a means of war propaganda. The work as a whole could be described as a history of the relation of cinema technology to war and, in particular, of the way in which cinema, as an industrial form, becomes deeply intertwined, throughout the twentieth century, with diverse aspects of industrialized warfare. For instance the propaganda and military machine of the Third Reich are shown to be exemplary of an 'osmosis between industrial war and cinema' (Virilio 1989: 58). In relation to the Second World War Virilio is interested specifically in the manner in which the technologies of film and those of aerial warfare combine to make of war itself a powerful visual spectacle. Night-time bombing, with its incendiary explosives, searchlights and firestorms have an effect which is destructive of material space in a limited form but whose impact on those who bear witness to the spectacle may be far more profoundly destructive (as, for instance, with the attempt by the Germans during the *Blitzkrieg* of 1941 to create a firestorm around the centre of London and to destroy St Paul's Cathedral). In the Second World War, Virilio argues, military and cinematic technology combine to make of war a spectacle of special effects, one which is developed to its highest form in the later stage of the conflict in the Allied aerial bombing: 'With the allied aerial offensive on the great European cities, assault suddenly became a spectacle of sound and light, a series of special effects, an atmospheric projection destined to confuse the minds of a fearful population' (Virilio 1989: 78).

It is the fusion of spectacular and nocturnal aerial assault with the industrial technologies of cinema which will define the terms of what war will slowly become in the post-war period. This is a period during which 'the decisive importance of this "logistics of perception"' comes to the fore and one in which conflict 'is now a war of images and sounds which replaces the war of objects' (Virilio 1989: 4). In this context Virilio identifies the existence of a 'fourth front' in the waging of warfare, that is to say, a new front of attack and defence which comes to supplement, and perhaps even dominate, the first three attack fronts of land, sea and air. The symbiosis of industrial war and cinema which begins with the First World War, and which is then developed in the Second, leads to the systematic opening up of this fourth front in modern and contemporary warfare. For Virilio the manner in which the conflict with Iraq was fought in 1991 most clearly testifies to the dominant role played by the fourth front. In *Desert Screen*, published in French in 1991 shortly after the conflict, he suggests that the fourth front is 'the front of the weapons of communication, of instantaneous information or destruction, cancelling all military power over both the earth and sky' (Virilio 2005e: 2–3). By this account the waging of war by the United States and its allies in the earlier 1990s was not just the electronic warfare of precision-guided cruise missiles (or 'smart bombs' as they were called at the time), but also, and far more importantly, war came to be waged as 'information warfare'. Here the fourth front of communications is used systematically to manipulate the representation and spectacle of war for the achievement of military goals.

A more recent example of this could, of course, be found in the 'shock and awe' tactics deployed by the Pentagon prior to the ground invasion of Iraq by US and coalition forces in March 2003. Here the targeted bombing of key buildings and installations in central Baghdad was combined with the visual spectacle of nocturnal explosions broadcast live around the world. The strategy seemed clear: the Iraqi military forces and civilian population could be intimidated into a position of weakness through both an immediate (for those living in Baghdad itself) and a mediatized exposure to the all-powerful force of destruction wrought by cruise missiles. In a work published originally in 1999 and entitled *The Strategy of Deception* Virilio presciently notes: 'the aim is no longer so much to blow up a structure as to neutralise the *infrastructure* of the adversary by spreading a general breakdown and panic within and around him through the brutal interruption of all coherent and coordinated activity' (Virilio: 2000c, 54). The fourth front exploits all the resources of the modern media, what Virilio elsewhere has called the 'wave optics' of electromagnetic and radio-electric communications, in order to master the space of conflict and dominate the adversary.

Once again Virilio detects a convergence or conjunction within contemporary warfare between means of destruction (e.g. long-range precision-guided missiles and other overwhelming forms of air power) and means of communication. Just as, in the Second World War, the industrial capability of the war machine and that of the cinema conjoined to make of war a spectacle of sound and light, so here, in modern electronic warfare, technologies of communication and weaponry combine: the war is played out as much on CNN and other broadcast media as it is in the specific theatre itself. At the same time it is controlled electronically from a central planning centre through the instantaneous control offered by electronic or digital data transmission. This is what Virilio dubs '*total electronic war*', a conjunction of media, communications and high-tech weaponry which 'leads to the supremacy of the *fourth front*', whereby 'the *pure* arms of communications and of instantaneous control of operations henceforth prevails over the other three fronts' (Virilio 2005e: 85).

The implications of war conceived of as '*total electronic war*' are at once military and political. The most important consequence that Virilio himself deduces from the dominance of the fourth front relates to the experience of time in both the military and the political spheres. He argues that the temporality of instantaneous data transmission, be it the transmission of weapons control or that of spectacular images of destruction, is such that the temporal delays which allow careful decision making and strategic thinking come to be eroded. This is felt first and foremost in the experience of command and control of combat situations themselves, where the control screen takes on a primary role:

> The screen becomes, therefore, the telescopic sight for a war where the attention of each is mobilized, whether he likes it or not. The horizon of the control monitor supplants both the military communiqué and the press, that mainstream press still necessary for analysis and reflection.
> (Virilio 2005e: 21)

The temporality of instantaneous transmission of data is such that the instant of the reflex reaction necessarily dominates the period of time in which considered analysis and reflection might occur (and this recalls, of course, the temporality of *exposure* discussed in previous chapters). This may have an impact, not just on the carrying out of military strategy and decision making, but on the nature of broader political consciousness: 'In this epoch military industrial and scientific logistics will prevail over strategic doctrines and truly political arguments. . . . The era opens as weapons of instantaneous communication come to dominate, thanks to globalized information networks and telesurveillance' (Virilio 2005e: 7). Just as the total war of 1940–45 and the total peace which followed it transformed the nature of geopolitical space by rendering obsolete the fortification of frontiers, so, according to Virilio, *total electronic war* transforms the nature of political time by eclipsing the temporality of delay and duration which, he argues, makes the reflection and developed argumentation of any true politics worthy of the name possible.

Unlike his friend and fellow thinker of the war and media, Jean Baudrillard, Virilio does not claim that the Gulf War did not take place (Baudrillard 1995: 61–87). Rather he suggests that the primary consequence of information and electronic warfare (that is, war waged predominantly on the fourth front of communications) is to alter the nature of the 'taking place' of military and political events *per se*. At the beginning of this discussion it was argued that, for Virilio, the remains of the Second World War bunkers on the Atlantic seaboard testified to the military obsolescence of frontiers and therefore to the passing of an era in which war was waged over the geopolitics of national borders. This, in turn, inaugurated the era of deterrence, that of total peace and pure war, in which a military and techno-scientific logic came to dominate political life at a fundamental level. It was also shown that Virilio traces a history of the interaction of war and cinema in their industrial form, one which sees war develop into a visual spectacle and then into the multimedia electronic war where communications and broadcast technologies combine to form a 'fourth front' which dominates the first three fronts of land, sea and air. The development of both pure war and of the fourth front is deeply rooted in emergent technologies of warfare and the impact these have on the structuring of military and political space. Above all Virilio appears to be concerned that the new technologies of electronic control, instantaneous data transfer and broadcast media inaugurate a progressive diminution of the experience of real space in favour of the real time of live transmission. His analysis of war appears to repeat, albeit in another form, his analysis of virtualization and the impact of modern media as outlined in the preceding chapter: 'Real time, that is to say the absolute speed of electromagnetic exchanges, dominates real space, in other words the *relative speed* of exchanges of position, occasioned until now by offensive and defensive manoeuvres' (Virilio 2005e: 85).

To this extent it becomes clear that all of Virilio's arguments regarding perception, dromology, virtualization, war and politics are closely interlinked. The implications of what he has to say in one area are always worked out for others in a consistent, if not altogether systematic, fashion. This has been most evident in the inseparability of the military and the political in his writing to the extent that the discussion of politics which follows in the next chapter cannot be separated from the arguments relating to warfare which have been discussed here. When Virilio analyses the structure and the importance of the fourth front in *Desert Screen* his concern is as much with the nature of contemporary politics as it is with military matters. As he himself puts it: 'The unique merit of the Persian Gulf war will therefore have been that of summoning us to respond politically to the challenge of real time' (Virilio 2005e: 93).

SUMMARY

The account Virilio gives of war and its relation to politics is closely bound up with his interest in the urban and with the question space and spatial organization. Virilio locates the origin of the city in war and in the need to concentrate dwelling and other social activities in areas that can be defended (either by fortifications or natural geography). In so doing Virilio comes to invert Clausewitz's belief that war is the continuation of politics by other means. For Virilio all political activity has its origin in the capacity of war to shape geographical terrain into geopolitical territory. Virilio initially develops his analysis in his first work, *Bunker Archeology*, arguing that the concrete fortifications of the Second World War mark a historical threshold. These fortifications, rendered redundant by the advent of systematic aerial bombing of urban centres, testify to a transformation in the geopolitical significance of territorial frontiers. This process of transformation is continued in the logic of nuclear deterrence which dominates the post-war period. According to Virilio the logic of deterrence governs the state of what he calls Total Peace and, later, Pure War. Both these terms stand as figures for a state of international security based in the generalized insecurity of civilian populations living under the threat of nuclear war. This state of insecurity leads to the suppression of the distinction between war and peace and underpins the evolution of the state as a highly militarized techno-scientific form of organization. Virilio also traces the role of technology in war by analysing the role of new visual media in modern warfare. From the importance of aerial photography and cinema technology in the two World Wars, through to the decisive role played by modern satellite and digital media in contemporary war, Virilio identifies a convergence between means of destruction and means of communication. This convergence determines the emergence of what Virilio calls the fourth front. After land, sea and air, the fourth front of electronic control and media communications has become the dominant terrain upon which contemporary battles are fought.

5

POLITICS

Political space and political time

Locating Virilio within any traditional or easily recognizable political position can appear to be a somewhat difficult task. At the very beginning of Chapter 1 it was indicated that he described himself in an interview as an 'anarcho-Christian' (Armitage 2001: 20). In the same interview he also claimed that he would happily adopt the labels 'communard' or 'anarcho-syndicalist' (Armitage 2001: 19). On this basis it can be argued that Virilio's politics may best be thought of as belonging to the French nonconformist, or non-Marxist, left. This claim runs counter to that made by Steve Redhead, who in *Paul Virilio: Theorist for an Accelerated Culture* describes Virilio in unequivocal terms as a liberal humanist (Redhead 2004: 125, 127, 129). According to Redhead, Virilio's politics would be more or less indistinguishable from 'a fairly standard liberal democratic position on democracy and electoral politics' (Redhead 2004: 127). What follows will argue that, although it is certainly right to call Virilio a humanist, the specific form his humanism takes is rather different from that of a conventional political liberal. Whilst he does indeed endorse the value of a certain idea of democracy, his humanism leads him to be highly critical of the contemporary liberal democratic state, and shapes his politics into a form which is decisively different from many aspects of conventional liberalism.

That Virilio is far from being a conventional liberal is borne out by his early involvement in the Catholic worker-priest movement in the early

1950s and his close association with figures such as Abbé Pierre (an involvement to which he alludes in the above-mentioned interview (Armitage
2001: 19)). In fact Virilio's politics cannot be explained with reference to
the terms 'conservative' or 'liberal' such as they might be familiar to us in
the Anglo-American or English-speaking political tradition. They should,
rather, be understood in relation to the personalist movement in France and
the thinking of personalism developed during the 1930s by Emmanuel
Mounier, who founded the influential Catholic review *Esprit* in 1932.
Personalism was a political doctrine which set itself squarely against what it
would call 'bourgeois liberalism', individualism and industrial capitalism.
It was also very much opposed to totalitarianism in all its forms and opposed
also to the technological ordering of the modern state. Against this it sought
to promote the notion of a community organized according to the value
of the person, that is a community in which persons and personal relations
would form the key point of reference (rather than, say, notions of technological or scientific progress, economic activity or abstract notions of
rights). Much of Virilio's thinking about politics is consistent with Mounier's
personalist thought or can be seen as a development of its key concerns and
values. Both the politics of the worker-priest movement in which the young
Virilio participated and that of his philosophical mentor, Maurice Merleau-
Ponty, were deeply marked by personalism. Without a familiarity with this
form of thinking, which sets itself squarely against the modern technological
state, bourgeois liberalism and industrial capitalism, it is difficult to properly
identify or evaluate the nature of Virilio's political positions or make much
sense of his political outlook more generally.

At the same time it should be recalled that, for Virilio, politics has its roots
in the space of the city (that is, of the *polis*) and that, as was shown in the
preceding chapter, the space of the city is in turn shaped by military space.
Any attempt to evaluate the political dimension of Virilio's writing has also
to bear in mind that he writes, not as a sociologist, political scientist or
political philosopher, but as an urbanist and as a dromologist (Armitage
2001: 173). His interest is to interrogate political structures, politics and the
nature of the political more generally from the perspective of speed, where
speed is taken as 'the categorical imperative of the modern world' or 'the
determining element, the absolute element' (Armitage 2001: 83–4). As
this study has indicated from the very beginning, Virilio is above all interested in space and movement, and, when it comes to politics, he is above all
interested in geopolitics and geostrategy in so far as it is shaped by spatial
organization and vectors of movement through space (Armitage 2001: 173).

What follows, then, will address the question of politics in Virilio's writing from the perspectives which are most important for him, namely that of the structuring of space and of the experience of time. Both of these are shaped at a fundamental level by the different possibilities of movement or transmission offered by changing technologies of transport and communications. Whether it be the space of the city, the state or of global geopolitical space, or the accelerated time of modern 'chronopolitics', speed remains for Virilio 'the determining element'. A number of commentators have tended to be somewhat critical in their judgements of Virilio's politics. For some his outlook remains too aesthetic, 'abstracted from political or any from of social concerns' (Leach in Armitage 2000: 81). For others, such as Douglas Kellner, his understanding of technology and of the technological state is flawed – 'excessively negative and one-sided' – and ignores 'the empowering and democratizing aspects of new computer and media technologies' (Armitage 2000: 103). The implication of such comments is perhaps that Virilio's approach is ultimately a little conservative or reactionary with respect to technology and the diversity of social forms to which technological innovation gives rise. The aim of this discussion will be less to criticize Virilio's political outlook than to highlight its specificity. Virilio's 'anarcho-Christian' nonconformist leftism may not be persuasive to many of his readers, yet arguably what counts is the different critical light that this outlook can shed on modern political and geopolitical realities.

POLITICAL SPACE

In the account given of *Bunker Archeology* in the previous chapter it was argued that, for Virilio, military space and political space were closely intertwined and, ultimately, inseparable. The obsolescence of frontier fortifications brought about by the advent of aerial bombing heralded the redundancy of national frontiers as defensive boundaries, and with that the eventual transformation of geopolitical realities by the logic of nuclear deterrence, total peace and then pure war. Much of Virilio's early work is, like *Bunker Archeology*, focused on the manner in which, throughout history, geographical terrain comes to exist as geopolitical territory by means of the technologies of penetration, defence and control, exerted within the military sphere. In many ways his first four works (*Bunker Archeology* published in 1975, *The Insecurity of Territory* in 1976, *Speed and Politics*, 1977, and *Popular Defence and Ecological Struggles*, published in 1978) represent an extended, if rather unstructured, meditation on the impact of military logistics and speeds of transmission on the shaping of political space throughout the course of history up to the second half of the twentieth century. Across these works Virilio gives an account of the importance of transport and communications in the birth and development of the city or the *polis*, and argues that the state as a political entity has its origins in the possibilities afforded by means of passing through, controlling and surveying geographical terrain. His analyses begin with the insistence that, as he puts it in *The Insecurity of Territory*, 'it must be recognized that politics is in the first instance a place: the City of earlier times, the community, then the project of the nation' (Virilio 1993: 152).

If politics, in the first instance, is a place or space, it is first and foremost a space which is *constructed*, that is to say, one which is controlled and shaped in certain ways. It may be recalled here that Virilio traced the origin of war to the abandonment of more or less spontaneous conflict at a certain point in history and to the subsequent adoption of military strategic thinking and planning around possibilities of attack and defence which, in its essence, were seen to be a matter of movement through space. If, according to Virilio's speculative history, the birth of the city can be more decisively located in the fortification of concentrated dwelling space than in the activities of trade and commerce, then the birth of political territory, and eventually that of the state itself, occurs as a result of artificial activity, or rather, of an artificial construction of space. This key point is made, somewhat elliptically, towards the beginning of *The Insecurity of Territory*: 'the birth of the State occurs precisely in the installation of its own being, that is to say, in the construction of the artificiality of its own field in the very heart of the field of sociality' (Virilio 1993: 80). The state, then, exists only as the result of a transformation of geographical terrain into an artificially constructed field which constitutes geopolitical territory. In this context military space precedes political space simply because it is military logistics, that of defence, attack, the surveying and control of geographical terrain which, according to Virilio, is the precondition for any artificial construction of space constitutive of geopolitical territory. It is not that Virilio has a particularly rigid or essentialist idea of the primacy of military affairs over civilian or political affairs *per se*. It is simply that he places the organization of space and the possibilities of movement through space according to relative speeds in a primordial position in relation to all other instances of organization. Being constructed on the basis of the control and penetration of space, and movement through space, the state, for Virilio, is dromocratic by nature, and is always, by definition, a project of mastery, as he puts it in *Speed and Politics*: 'For the dromocratic State, mastery over the earth is already the mastery over its dimensions' (Virilio 1986: 70).

It is in this context that Virilio's critical understanding of the state, or what might even be called his 'anti-statism', needs to be understood. It is also within this context that his humanist perspective becomes most apparent. Since the project of state formation is, above all, one of the control and mastery of space, it is not, for Virilio, a project which is necessarily orientated towards the human individual or one which takes the human person as its principal measure. When Virilio talks about the state, about its origins and about the history of its formation he is principally talking about the rise of the state in Europe and what he calls the 'Western state' (although the theoretical question of movement through, and control of, space could, of course, be posed in relation to the development of non-Western states). Broadly speaking he speaks positively about the ancient model of the city-state or *polis*, describing it in *Negative Horizon* as 'the political site *par excellence*' (Virilio 2005a: 77). The city-state or *polis* – and by this should be understood the pre-modern formation of an urban political centre controlling rural hinterland – appears to offer Virilio a model of political community which is more properly adjusted to the scale of human interaction than the various forms of state organization which succeeded it. Indeed, he describes the rise of the modern state in terms which implicitly oppose it to the ancient city-state or *polis*. The formation of the modern state is, according to this account, a project which seeks not only to survey and control space, but also to exert an ever more total mastery over it. It has the extension of its own field as its only goal or purpose and, 'in achieving its totality', it bypasses the measure of the human altogether or, as Virilio puts it: 'its relations to the "human model" are entirely modified' (Virilio 1993: 57). In effect he sees the modern state as developing according to a logic which is inimical to the needs of the human: 'The rise of the Western state is nothing other than the expansion of its own being against all other existing things' (Virilio 1993: 81).

This tendency of the state to affirm its own existence and the necessities of that existence over those of other existing things is exacerbated, or perhaps, Virilio might contend, is brought to its most extreme point in the development of the modern technological state. For Virilio 'the technological STATE needs the human moment only in a very secondary manner, since it represents something which gets in the way of its functioning' (Virilio 1993: 54). Virilio's thinking about contemporary politics and geopolitics cannot be understood without reference to his conception of the state as a field of totalizing (dromocratic) control and mastery, on the one hand, and as an entity which expands itself according to a logic which is alien to the ends of the human on the other. It is at this fundamental level of a specific conceptualization of state power that his humanism, or rather his privileging of the human person as a measure of value, plays a decisive role. The influence of personalism on Virilio is arguably very important here. Personalism, as a form of thought which affirms the primacy of the human person and personal human relations as the end or goal of political community, was from its inception in the 1930s anti-totalitarian, anti-fascist and anti-communist, but also and at the same time set itself against modern industrial capitalism and the ideology of 'bourgeois' liberalism which underpins it. In other words personalism set itself against all those modern forms of political ideology and organization which sought to subsume the individual person into impersonal processes: the one-party (Nazi or communist) state on the one hand or the reign of industrial capital on the other.

This strain of personalist thinking runs through the account of technological modernity given by Virilio and shapes his political response to it. The following passage from *The Insecurity of Territory* which describes the space of a modern city is typical of his outlook:

> The squares and roads, cluttered up with cars, are empty of humanity like those like those of a city of the end of the world. . . . Technological power has installed itself in this desynchronization of our consciousness without us having realized it, because above and beyond an image of power devoid of people, it is the image of the disappeared citizen which is hidden in the city but no longer shows itself, it hides in buildings, motor cars, and behind the functioning of administration and its world of instruments.
>
> (Virilio 1993: 58–9)

To many readers such assertions may appear to be all too sweeping and far too negative in their rejection of the way in which modern urban and social spaces are permeated with diverse technologies. Certainly comments such as this reflect what has been highlighted in previous chapters as Virilio's potentially catastrophist or apocalyptic tone, a tone which may imply an exaggerated pessimism in his overall outlook. Once again it seems evident that, for Virilio, the driving force of technological modernity and the political forms to which it gives rise are overwhelmingly opposed to the dimension of the human person which he seeks to affirm. As he begins his writing career in the 1970s with works such as *Bunker Archeology*, *The Insecurity of Territory* and *Speed and Politics*, his perspective is defined by the feeling that 'What is currently in process . . . is *the definitive, one could say final, reduction of human society by the Western state*' (Virilio 1993: 129). It would be easy in the light of such comments to reproach Virilio for his excessive negativity with regard to technology or, like Nicholas Zurbrugg, to criticize his 'tendency to hide – and virtually obliterate – all traces of positive technological practices' (Armitage 2000: 193). There is a sense in which, ultimately, readers of Virilio have to judge for themselves how they respond to his personalist vision, a vision which is, in a way, personal to him, and certainly very particular to a specific moment in the nonconformist politics of the Christian left in France during the pre- and post-Second World War period.

However one might respond to this personalist dimension of Virilio's political thinking, what is arguably of interest in his various analyses is the manner in which they invite his readers to question or respond critically to key aspects of technological society and the political organization of the technological state. Some of the most original and compelling insights he offers relate, as might now be expected, to the way in which speeds of transmission (of transport and communications) have an impact on the distribution of power within the state and on the structure of the state itself. Virilio questions whether the diminishing of distances or the 'supraconductivity of different milieux' offered by high-speed transport and quasi-instantaneous communications is not also, 'along with the power of concentration, the concentration of power' (Virilio 1993: 129). The important question he raises relates, then, to the way in which technological innovation may be in the process of changing the nature and distribution of power in modern liberal democratic states. As always Virilio approaches this question from the perspective of the modes by which the structures of space and of temporal experience are organized. He is concerned with the transformation of geopolitical space and, with that, the changing nature of political temporality in contemporary life. As will become clear he even questions whether our ideal of democracy, or indeed its actually existing institutions, can sustain themselves in the 'real time' of high-speed communications and broadcast media.

As his writing develops during the 1980s and 1990s in works such as *The Lost Dimension*, *Negative Horizon* (both published originally in 1984) and

Open Sky (published in 1995), Virilio increasingly focuses on the changing political significance of urban space. He focuses also on the way in which urban transformation is accompanied by changes in global geopolitical organization. In this context he sees the increased speeds of transmission of modern transport and communications as having a negative impact on the political significance of urban centres. This leads to a specific kind of de-urbanization which he describes in the following terms:

> the *Polis* is no longer the political site *par excellence*, the delocalization of the means of communication initiates a poorly understood phenomenon of de-urbanization, since it does not yet strike visibly at the site of the metropolitan concentration. The social and political problem of populations is translated from the place to the non-place of exchanges and of quasi-instantaneous migrations; *the state of emergency becomes the new city of a sort populating of time, in that 'place' where the state of siege once determined the populating of space.*
>
> (Virilio 2005a: 77)

This is not a de-urbanization which involves the physical emptying out of populations. What is at stake here is rather the changing nature of what one might call the *site* of politics or of political activity. Virilio is suggesting that, with the development of modern transport and communications, the political space of the city is diminished in favour of a dimension which is temporal rather than spatial. He describes a development within the sphere of politics which is identical to that described in relation to the 'becoming virtual' of experience discussed in Chapter 3. Once again the accelerated rapidity of transport and the instantaneity of telecommunications are viewed as a negation of the space, volume or extension of the world. If, for Virilio, politics has its origin in the space of the *polis*, and the *polis* or city originates, in turn, in the military planning of space, then the waning importance of the spatial extension which is brought about by accelerated speeds of transmission necessarily has a fundamental impact on political life. In this context the city ceases to be a material space whose political significance lies primarily in the mastery of its spatial dimensions. The space of the *polis* is no longer fundamentally orientated around the control of the city itself, the defence of its limits and strategic centres of power (the palace, parliament, government buildings etc.). In the latter half of the twentieth century, Virilio contends, urban space loses 'its geopolitical reality in favour of systems of instantaneous transmission' (Virilio 1991a:

16). The 'place' of politics is less the material space of urban terrain and far more the virtual 'place' of communications and the temporality of real time proper to them.

POLITICAL TIME

This shift in the site of the political from the spatial dimension of the *polis* or city to the temporal dimension of high-speed or instantaneous exchanges, transmissions and communications has, according to Virilio, shaped the key developments in political culture, ideology and power structures in the technological societies of the late twentieth century. For instance, it is this shift towards what he comes to call 'chronopolitics' which, he contends, underpins the rise to dominance of ideologies of the minimal state, free markets, privatization and deregulation in the last three decades of that century. As early as 1978 Virilio describes the 'MINIMUM STATE' promoted by those he dubs 'anarcho-capitalists' as a 'STATE which can only appear as MINIMUM to the extent that its sphere of influence is not that of a more or less inert territorial body but that of a body of ceaselessly active communications which is nevertheless invisible and unknowable' (Virilio 1990: 94). In *Negative Horizon* he develops this idea in more detail:

> The past and the future of the economy of the management of time replaces what is proximally in front and behind in the management of space; with the advent of this instantaneity, power moves toward a hypothetical centre of time, an axis of convergence of an absolute mobilization where the intensive succeeds the extensive and where the *maximum state, the providence state*, gives way suddenly to the *minimum state, the destiny state*.
>
> (Virilio 2005a: 78)

The language of intensivity and extensivity used here is the same as that used by Virilio to articulate his thinking about light-time, the temporality of exposure, and the virtualization of experience discussed in Chapters 2 and 3. Rather than being applied to the temporality of embodied perception or collective experience mediated by modern communications, this language now emerges as the key to understanding political developments. Effectively Virilio is offering a critical explanation for the decline in ideologies of state control, the shift way from the politics of big government and the rise of neo-liberal economics. According to this account, the crisis of faith in government ownership, intervention and management of society, which has characterized the recent politics of economically advanced nations, is not simply a result of the end of the Cold War, or of the collapse of ideologies of the left. Neither is it a result of politics simply keeping up with perceived necessities of technological 'progress'. From his earliest works Virilio is, as one might expect, sharply critical of ideologies of progress which aim to subordinate all political and social developments to technological innovation (e.g. Virilio 1993: 122). The move away from what he calls the 'maximum' or 'providence' state is far more a result of the way in which modern technologies alter the fundamental spatial and temporal structuring of the site or place of politics. Here it is the time of quasi-instantaneous communications, exchanges and data transfer which defines the space or site of the *polis* and with this comes the politics of electronic markets and global capital flows and the minimal state structure which is necessary for the management of this virtual space of the political.

Indeed, Virilio extends this argument even further by suggesting that it is not just the politics of the minimal state which is inaugurated in the becoming virtual of political space. The boundaries, limits, and interrelation of states with each other have also, Virilio argues, been radically transformed. As the space of the city is diminished in significance and the site of political activity shifts towards the virtual realm of data transfer and communications, the minimal state which issues from this transformation is no longer primarily rooted in the geographical reality of national populations. The temporal dimension which comes to define it, that is to say, real-time communication, is a-national and constituted primarily in its connections and interconnections with other key points of communication situated in diverse centres across the globe. Virilio expresses this in the following terms:

> Hyperconnected in these terminal points and other control and surveillance points, the anational State prepares to cast off its moorings with urban populations, its milieu is henceforth the non-lieu, the non-place, of speed, the non-territory of an essentially vectorial politics where the pre-eminence of Time replaces that of Space.
>
> (Virilio 2005a: 95)

Comments such as these suggest that Virilio is offering, not just an account of the triumph of markets and global capital flows within the politics of the late twentieth and early twenty-first centuries. He also offers an account of the broader forces underpinning globalization throughout this period. In *The Information Bomb* he describes globalization as 'the great GLOBALITARIAN mutation' and as a 'Global delocalization which effects the very nature of identity' (Virilio 2000a: 10). In this mutation of the state and its unmooring from the extension of geopolitical territory, from its frontiers and urban centres, the very idea of a 'nation-state' orientated around a people sharing an identity and a territory is thrown into question more than ever before. What counts in this new global geopolitical field described by Virilio is not so much cities as political centres, or territorial borders as political frontiers, but the interconnection of information centres. These centres may themselves be important cities (e.g. Paris, London, New York, Tokyo etc.) but what counts is the manner in which they are hooked up to form something like a global information-city in comparison with which the actual and material extension of the city itself is nothing but a local suburb. Virilio describes this process at some length in *The Information Bomb*:

> The LOCAL CITY is already nothing but a DISTRICT, one arrondissement amongst others of the invisible GLOBAL METACITY whose *centre is everywhere and circumference nowhere*.
>
> A virtual hypercentre, of which real cities are only ever the periphery, this phenomenon accentuates even more, along with the desertification of rural space, the decline of average cities, which are unable to resist for very long the attraction of metropoles which have at their disposal the totality of telecommunications facilities as well as high speed aerial or terrestrial transport links.
>
> (Virilio 2000a: 11)

The globalized world is, according to Virilio, one in which the territorially orientated industrial and political complex of nineteenth-century and early twentieth-century capitalism is succeeded by a globally extended informational and metropolitical complex sustained by the high speeds of transport and electromagnetic data transmission. This is not a political situation defined by the opposition between an industrial capital-owning class and an industrial proletariat. The division in this new global field is between those who are connected to the new real-time *polis* or meta-city and those who are excluded from it (Virilio 2005b, 95). The difference, then, is not simply a spatial difference, for instance between those in the 'Third World' or developing countries and those in the 'First World' or developed countries. Virilio's claim is that traditional geopolitical structures of global space have changed in so far as what counts is the concentration of power, information and economic activity into (technologically empowered) nodal points distributed variably across the globe. Here the former distinction of, say, metropolitan centre (e.g. Europe, the United States) and colonial or post-colonial (e.g. Africa, South America) periphery is subtly modified, since what is important is whether one participates in the technological community of 'real-time' (i.e. quasi-instantaneous) informational and economic/financial activity or whether one is excluded from it. Examples of this phenomenon would not be difficult to find. One need only think, for instance, of all those who labour in the fields, factories, sweatshops and mines of the former colonial centres while the elites of those same countries work in digitally connected and Western-style urban districts (with their high-tech skyscrapers and office buildings, often situated in close proximity to makeshift slums or shanty towns).

It should be clear from this that Virilio is not suggesting that the modern globalized world is without inequality. Nor, as has been indicated, is he seeking to defend the forces of globalization and of modern capitalism by asserting the inevitability of technological progress. As always, his analysis aims to uncover a more or less hidden dimension of spatial and temporal organization, to account for its vectors of movement, speeds of transmission and overall impact on our collective experience and organization of space and time. As has been argued throughout this study, it is only on this basis that a critical response to the hidden tendencies of technological innovation and development can become possible and that a politics which diverges from technocratic orthodoxies (of free markets, privatization, deregulation etc.) can emerge.

Indeed, Virilio refers to the regime of 'real time' which governs the global meta-city of information exchanges as a *'tyranny of real time'* (Virilio 1993: 283). His concern is certainly with the global inequalities that persist in this new order of chronopolitics. It is also with the way in which the temporal dimension of instantaneity and intensivity proper to the high-speed transmission of information leads to a wasting of the political culture of democracy. One of the dominant concerns of Virilio's analysis of modern chronopolitics is the question of whether the virtual *polis* of real time, and the meta-city to which it gives rise, is a site which is in any way compatible with anything which might properly resemble a democratic polity. In a postscript to the 1993 reprint of *The Insecurity of Territory* Virilio invokes the possibility that whatever democracy we do have may 'disappear with the advent of a new tyranny, the *tyranny of real time*, which would no longer permit democratic control, but only the conditioned reflex, *automatism*' (Virilio 1993: 283). He repeats this point in an interview with Philippe Petit published in 1996:

> The tyranny of real time is not very different from classical tyranny, because it tends to liquidate the reflective capacity of the citizen in favour of a reflex action. Democracy is about solidarity, not solitary experience, and humans need time to reflect before acting. Yet the real time and global present requires on the part of the telespectator a reflex response which is already of the order of manipulation.
>
> (Virilio 1999: 87)

However pessimistic or negative his analysis may appear to some, it is arguable that Virilio's thinking about the 'tyranny of real time' addresses very real concerns about the nature of contemporary democracy which have become increasingly widespread in the early twenty-first century. In particular the mediatization of political and electoral campaigns has been a central source of anxiety or malaise in this context. For instance the close relations of the UK Labour Party leadership with the media tycoon Rupert Murdoch during the 1990s and the first years of the new millennium led many to question how much political influence lies with unelected corporate interests rather than the voters themselves. Of even more concern has been the role played by Sylvio Berlusconi in Italian politics, where the owner of a corporate empire controlling substantial portions of the national broadcast media was, until early 2006, also the leader of the ruling party *and* Prime Minister. Likewise in the United States the question of the relation between the government of George W. Bush, business and corporate media interests (in particular those of Rupert Murdoch) have been constantly raised in one form or another since the first electoral 'success' of this government in 2000. (Indeed, it has been argued that the Bush administration itself is composed of nothing other than the representatives of business and corporate interests.) In 1976 Virilio asked whether the 'supraconductibility of milieux' proper to modern communications did not also entail 'the concentration of power' (Virilio 1993: 266). In 2006, at the time of writing this study, questions about the shift of power and influence from democratic institutions (e.g. the elected government, parliament) to unelected corporate interests and technocratic administrative bodies arise more frequently than ever.

Yet, as the above quotation makes clear, Virilio is not concerned simply with the concentration of power and influence in the hands of small elites. (This is arguably nothing new in capitalist liberal democratic societies.) Rather he is concerned with the way in which this enhanced influence of corporate interests has its source in the nature of the virtual space of the *polis* itself and the intensive temporality of 'real time'. The real tyranny, for Virilio, or the source of corporate media power and its attendant interests, lies in the way in which experience is constructed or structured within modern broadcast media. Here Virilio's analysis of political life rejoins his analysis of telepresence, the culture of tele-spectacle, and of the tele-image discussed at the end of Chapter 3. In this context, it may be recalled, he pointed, in works such as *The Vision Machine*, to the emergence of 'new industrialisation of vision, the putting into place of a veritable market of synthetic perception' (Virilio 1994b: 59). It is not perhaps, that the media tycoons of today control or manipulate collective opinion and perception in exactly the same manner as did the propaganda of the totalitarian states of the early twentieth century. Rather it is that the shaping and synchronization of collective perception and experience in the virtual world of telepresence is necessarily an artificial construction or representation. In turn the general world view or outlook of those holding media power will necessarily tend to shape the nature of that construction or representation. A good example of this might be the impact of Rupert Murdoch's hostility to the European Union and the influence of his media outlets on UK public opinion. Whatever deep-seated historical hostilities towards Europe that may exist within the British population, it is arguable that the anti-European tone of the Murdoch print press in particular worked to shape a specifically con-temporary form of anti-European sentiment in the 1980s, 1990s and early twenty-first century. Both directly and indirectly, this may have had an impact on UK accession to the European single currency in the creation of a climate of opinion which made the holding of a referendum on the single currency a politically suicidal act for those running the government.

More important still, for Virilio at least, is the manner in which the intensive temporality of virtual presence or telepresence is not one of duration and more or less reasoned debate and exchange but, as has been indicated, one of emotion and reflex reaction. In *City of Panic* he expresses this in the following terms:

> We today face the threat, no longer simply of a democracy of opinion which would replace the representative democracy of political parties, but

the excess of a veritable DEMOCRACY OF EMOTION; of a collective emotion, simultaneously synchronised and globalised, whose model could well be that of *a post-political televangelism*.

(Virilio 2005b: 37)

The risk is that modern broadcast media have ushered in an 'era of synchronization' where what may appear to be our individual opinions, views or emotions are shaped by the forces of an industrialized vision and perception and the temporality of the instant, and of instant response, which belongs to the virtual realm of telepresence. A concrete example of this might be the way in which, within the contemporary politics of the United Kingdom, government ministers are often accused of forming policy, and in particular policies on immigration, asylum, law and order, on a more or less *ad hoc* basis and in response to campaigns or pressure from the broadcast media or the mediatized culture of the news press. This is, of course, always denied. However Virilio's thinking around the question of democracy, and of the 'democracy of emotion', offers an important theoretical perspective from which a deeper understanding of what is at stake in the contemporary interplay between politics, media, and the shifting balances of power and influence in a digital age of information technology.

Despite his resolutely personalist perspective, Virilio does not give an explicit or programmatic account of what kind of politics we should adopt if we wish to refuse or react politically to the situation he describes. In this context his writing is analytical rather than prescriptive, it aims to reveal hidden tendencies rather than dictate our responses to them. In this case his overall account of the place of the political and the emergence of chronopolitics aims to reveal a hidden and fundamental dimension of an increasingly technocratic political culture. This virtual space of real time and telepresence is the space of a technical culture and infrastructure which, for Virilio, forms the contemporary site of political activity. He warns unequivocally that 'there is no democratisation of this technical culture' (Virilio 1999: 33).

However Virilio's readers may respond to his personalist politics, and whatever their own politics may be, it is his dromological perspective which is arguably of greatest interest and importance. Despite the fragmented or seemingly *ad hoc* nature of Virilio's writing, all the various moments of his thinking about politics interlink to form a coherent vision. The decline in the political significance of the city or *polis* is accompanied by the rise of globalization and the informational interconnectedness of the global meta-city. The decline in the political significance of territorial space and national frontiers is accompanied by the rise of the minimum state and the ideology of free markets, privatization and deregulation. The decline in ideologies of state ownership is accompanied by the increasing concentration of power and influence in unelected corporate and technocratic elites who manage the virtual dimension of real-time exchanges. Finally the rise of these elites is accompanied by the ascendancy of a democracy of synchronized emotion where real debate and ideological difference are increasingly displaced in favour of sound-bites and reflex responses. Virilio's political outlook may at times appear too pessimistic or negative. However, as a dromological analysis engaging with fundamental structures of spatial and temporal organization, it offers strikingly original insights whose force and penetration make them indispensable for any attempt to understand the forces at work in the political realities of the early twenty-first century.

SUMMARY

Virilio's politics need to be understood against the background of his early involvement with the Catholic worker-priest movement of the 1950s and in the context of the politics of personalism developed by Emmanuel Mounier in the 1930s. The doctrines of personalism inform Virilio's anti-statist tendency and his critical understanding of the role of technology in modern political and social organization. Virilio's thinking about politics and the political calls into question the way in which the abolition of distance brought about by modern transport and communications have an impact on the structure of political space and, in particular, have come to shape the nature of the modern liberal democratic state and have influenced the progress of globalization. Virilio describes a shift whereby the spatial dimension of territorial geopolitics is displaced in favour of a temporal dimension of 'chrono-politics' understood as the management of real-time information exchanges, market activity and flows of global capital. According to Virilio the rise of chronopolitics underpins the rise of neo-liberal economics and the politics of minimal statism. It also has shaped the restructuring of global space normally referred to as globalization.

Virilio also calls into question the way in which modern chronopolitics, and broadcast media, may lead to a wasting of democracy and democratic political institutions and processes.

6

ART

The accident of art

Virilio's interest in the relation of technology to the development of art and artistic practices in the twentieth century runs throughout his writing career. From his discourse on cinema in *The Aesthetics of Disappearance* (Virilio 1991b) and *War and Cinema* (Virilio 1989), to his meditation on painting in *Negative Horizon* (Virilio 2005) or his thinking of 'motorized' art in *The Art of the Motor* (Virilio 1995), he has persistently raised questions about the status of modern art and the impact of new technologies upon artistic technique and upon the plurality of artistic practice more generally. Indeed, it is arguable that such questions have become more dominant in his most recently published works and interviews, in, for instance *Art and Fear* (Virilio 2003b), *Discours sur l'horreur de l'art* (Virilio and Baj 2003), *The Accident of Art* (Virilio and Lotringer: 2005) and *L'Art à perte de vue* (Virilio 2005d). Despite this, relatively little critical attention has been given to the important role played by the plastic and visual arts in Virilio's discourse as a whole. This is perhaps because his account of modern art can, like other aspects of his thinking, initially appear to be rather negative and therefore of lesser interest to art critics, who perhaps necessarily engage with contemporary artistic production on the basis that it has a more positive value or worth. Virilio's discourse on art is, as will become clear, highly polemical and very critical of the contemporary state of the arts in Europe and the United States.

Yet, if he is polemical or critical in relation to the state of contemporary art, this is because he firmly believes that art itself exists as a critical or oppositional medium of expression and that this critical or oppositional function has all but disappeared from much of the artistic production of recent decades. Perhaps one of the most interesting aspects of Virilio's discourse on contemporary art is that he poses the question of the 'contemporary' itself in a critical fashion. For Virilio the question of the contemporary in art does not simply relate to the current state or development of new and innovative techniques which displace established forms and render them obsolete or passé. In so far as he poses this question he seeks to relate the current state of art to other phenomena, or, as he puts it in *Art and Fear*: 'A contemporary art, yes, but contemporary with what?' (Virilio 2003b: 27). We can respond to the question of art, Virilio asserts, only if we first engage with the *culture* of art, that is to say, with the wider world which shapes artistic production. It will not be surprising then that, for Virilio, the art of the late twentieth and early twenty-first centuries is perceived as being contemporary, in a decisive manner, with the technologies of speed, the culture of acceleration, and the becoming virtual of experience which have been discussed in previous chapters. What the art of this period has failed to do, he maintains, is develop a mode of expression which would be critical or oppositional in relation to this contemporary culture of speed, acceleration and virtualization. For Virilio, art is necessarily inserted into the world, or rather it arises and takes its life from the existence of the artist in the world. Art cannot, and should not, detach itself from the world and the diverse ways in which the world is subject to change. This means that it cannot and should not detach itself from situated bodily experience or what one might call the 'human sensorium' of embodied life. Virilio expresses this in the following terms: 'The work of art is not academic, it does not obey any preconceived design'; rather it expresses, 'the extreme vigilance of the living body which sees, hears, surmises, moves, breathes, changes' (Virilio 2002: 71). Once again the affirmation of a bodily perspective and the privileging of situated embodied experience lie at the centre of Virilio's concerns.

MODERN ART ON TRIAL

The historical account of twentieth-century art given by Virilio seeks to frame the wider culture of artistic production within a twofold perspective: that of war and that of the technological innovations of cinema, video and digital media. The account he gives is arguably a little bit schematic or reductive and is certain to be disputed by many. It is clear, though, that, in framing the history of modern art within this dual perspective, Virilio is aiming to relate artistic production to the way in which technological innovation has transformed our experience of the world.

In the first instance he refers to the cataclysmic events of the First and Second World Wars to explain the, often violent, disintegration of form and figurative techniques in modern art from cubism onwards. The fourth chapter showed the way in which, for Virilio, the two World Wars of the twentieth century were decisively marked by technological innovation: the development of shelling and indirect (photographic, cinematic) viewing of the battlefield in the case of the First World War, and the development of systematic aerial bombing of civilian populations in the Second. This ever increasing automation and mechanization of warfare inaugurated, Virilio argues, new forms of violence and horror which left their mark on the experience of the individual artists who fought, and on the culture of art more generally. In an interview with the Italian anarchist artist Enrico Baj he expresses this in the following terms: 'One cannot understand what happened after cubism, through to abstract art . . . , if one does not link it to the horrors of war, of wars which were rendered even more horrible by technology, by gas, by new bombs' (Virilio and Baj 2003: 47). By this account the violence done to form in the successive waves of avant-garde or modernist art is not just a critical gesture directed against the tradition or against received ways of seeing or representing the world. Rather the dissolution of form which characterized so much modern art was a response to, or rather, Virilio would say, was symptomatic of, the increasing extremities of violence permitted by new technologies of war. An obvious example of this link between the experience of war and artistic development would be the founding of the Dada movement during the First World War. The Dada movement was formed in Zurich in 1916 by, among others, Tristan Tzara (1896–1963), Jean Arp (1887–1966) and Hugo Ball (1886–1927). These artists and thinkers represented a younger generation who reacted strongly against the horrors of the war. Dadaism was a movement of revolt. It represented a revolt against conservative values and against the political powers of the day. The aim was to break with all received values and to destroy, terrorize and subvert. The targets of the Dadaists were artistic but also cultural and social. The extremity of their project, their desire to lay waste to all received forms of art and linguistic expression or meaning, arose as a direct result of the crisis in values precipitated by the horrors of the new mechanized warfare. A similar case could be made for the French surrealists, who in the immediate post-war period and very early 1920s were closely tied to the Dadaists. André Breton (1896–1966) was the leader of the surrealist group and had, like many artists and intellectuals of the period, experienced the war at first hand. The desire of surrealism was to destroy old cultural forms and systems of meaning in order to transform human experience and create new ways of being based on the liberation of unconscious desire. The dismemberment of form which occurs in surrealist and Dadaist works can arguably be related to the destruction of forms (bodies, landscapes and cityscapes) which characterized the violence of the First World War. Virilio himself lists a number of artists prominent in the twentieth-century avant-garde movements who participated directly in either the First or Second World War (Virilio and Baj 2003: 47). The violence done to form in modern art is, he argues, above all a violence done to the form of bodies or what Virilio calls 'the torture of bodies . . . the torture of the form of bodies, of all bodies' (Virilio and Baj 2003: 47). It is this violence against the body, taken to extremes in the mechanization of war and killing that defined so much of the twentieth century, that explains the rise of abstraction and the shift away from representation in twentieth-century art.

In parallel to this argument Virilio suggests that the development of modern cinema also had a decisive impact on the formal development of art, and, in particular, on that of the plastic arts. In Chapter 3 it was argued that his notion of the 'aesthetics of disappearance' described the manner in which cinema, unlike sculpture or painting, produced sensible forms which had no lasting material support (e.g. of stone or canvas and paint). According to this account the images of film, it will be recalled, exist only in the immateriality of light as it passes through celluloid and in the fleeting passage of the celluloid itself within the motorized mechanism of the projector. If, for Virilio, art is a medium which arises first and foremost from the sensory experience of human embodiment, then this loss of material durability in the work of art might easily have implications for the nature of artistic expression more generally, or, as Virilio puts it: 'the aesthetics of disappearance also contains the possibility of the disappearance of the aesthetic' (Virilio and Baj 2003: 25). The clear implication here is that the wider cultural impact of cinema's aesthetic of disappearance (that is, its impact on general structures of seeing and perception) will also be felt within the realm of artistic production. In *Art and Fear* Virilio expresses this in the following terms:

the invention of the CINEMATOGRAPH radically modified the experience of the *duration of exposure*, the temporal regime of plastic arts. During the last century the CINEMATIC aesthetic of disappearance supplanted the STATIC appearance which had existed in previous millennia.

(Virilio 2003b: 73)

It should be stressed that Virilio at no point dismisses the value of cinema as an artistic medium, nor does he suggest that, say, sculpture or painting are straightforwardly superior forms. Indeed, throughout his career he has engaged with or made reference to film makers of diverse periods within the twentieth century (for instance, early film makers such as Abel Gance (1889–1981) and René Clair (1898–1981) (in *The Aesthetics of Disappearance*), those of the pre- and post-Second World War period such as Michael Powell (1905–90) (in *The Art of the Motor*), or the contemporary Canadian film maker, Atom Egoyan (1960–). Rather he is suggesting that cinema, as a medium of appearance based on an aesthetic of disappearance, inaugurates a different logic within the more general space of artistic production, a logic that goes beyond the question of figuration, form or abstract expression which underpins his account of art and war. According to this different logic the representational function of art, that is, its capacity to *re-present* an image of the world, is replaced by a specific mode of 'presentation'. In one of his most recent texts, *Art as far as the Eye can see* (*L'Art à perte de vue*, Virilio 2005d), Virilio opposes 'representation in the real space of the work' to 'the pure and simple presentation, in real time, of events' (Virilio 2005d: 107). He also alludes elsewhere to what he calls the 'end of REPRESENTATIONAL art' and to the dominance of a 'PRESENTATIONAL art' (Virilio 2003b: 35). In effect he is suggesting that cinema inaugurates a mode of aesthetic experience where the presentation of image and form takes precedence over, and increasingly comes to obscure, the reality that the image or form may represent. Inaugurated by cinema, this mode of viewing is developed, Virilio adds, in subsequent technologies of video and digital imaging which emerge in the latter part of the twentieth century. This dominance of the presentational over the representational could be seen, for instance, in abstract art, where artistic figuration is entirely detached from the sensible forms of the world. It is arguably also present in, say, video installations or other techniques of modern art where the formal aspects of presentation lie at the centre of the aesthetic experience rather than any realistic or representational function (for instance in performance art or other types of installation art). This shift from representation to presentation is, for Virilio, an effect of 'the impact of technical and motorized arts upon the plastic arts of which cinema has been the vector, the canal' (Virilio and Baj 2003: 20).

The twofold perspective which underpins this account of modern art, that is, the impact of war on the one hand, and of motorized and technical media on the other, clearly serves, for Virilio, to explain the general movement within the twentieth century whereby art became more abstract and more detached from the techniques of figuration and representation. This movement is, from Virilio's perspective, problematic in a number of ways. If, as he asserts, art is inserted into the world and emerges from the sensory, embodied experience of the artist in the world, then the technization of art, and with this the increasing dominance of presentation at the expense of representation, would represent a narrowing of what art can do, a restriction of its scope and possibility. On one level this narrowing of possibility is manifest in the range of techniques open to art. Virilio the former stained glass artisan and collaborator with Henri Matisse and Georges Braque is clearly concerned that the technization of art may lead to a reduction in the plurality of artistic techniques:

> Motorized art, has, through video and digital art, contributed to the progressive elimination of a good number of representational techniques. It is not just the subject of painting which comes under attack but its technique, as is the case elsewhere with the techniques of engraving and of all the living arts.
>
> (Virilio and Baj 2003: 21)

His concern, then, is not to condemn, say, video art *per se*, but to question whether certain techniques tend to be privileged at the expense of others in a way which leads to the 'elimination of pluralism' (Virilio and Baj 2003: 20). Yet on another, perhaps more serious, level the narrowing of possibility within modern art manifests itself in the relation it maintains to the wider world, the world of culture, politics and events. Just as the techniques of art may become ever more restricted, so, Virilio argues, may its ability to engage critically with the dimension of collective human experience.

This argument is made at some length in *Art and Fear* (Virilio 2003b), a work published originally in French as *La Procédure silence* in 2000. As Virilio himself indicates this work proved to be highly controversial in France when it was first published and, in particular, drew criticism from much of the

French press (Virilio and Lotringer 2005: 21). The title of the original French appears in the English translation as 'Art on Trial'. Here the French *procédure* is taken as a judicial process or proceeding. In this sense art is on trial for what Virilio sees as the subtle self-censorship of much modern art in the face of the challenges posed by the modern world. It may be noted that *procédure* in French also refers to a method of proceeding or 'procedure' in the sense of a process undertaken. There is perhaps a play on meaning here. Art follows a procedure of silence or self-censorship and as such is put on trial. This potential culpability of art is underpinned by what, to many, would be a very straightforward political reality, namely 'THOSE WHO SAY NOTHING CONSENT' (Virilio 2003b: 74). According to Virilio modern and contemporary art has, in its obsession with the critical deconstruction of form, and in its preference for presentation over representation, fallen silent about the pressing realities of worldly experience. Virilio expresses this in the following terms: 'A victim of the *procedure of silence*, contemporary art has for a long time now sought to diverge, in other words, to practice CONCEPTUAL DIVERSION' (Virilio 2003b: 76). Rather than seek convergence with the world, art has sought, in a more or less continual and systematic fashion, to pursue strategies of divergence, whereby the figurative, conceptual and representational forms are subjected to ceaseless deformation and reformation. This, for Virilio, is an abrogation of a central responsibility of art, or, at the very least, a suppression of its fundamental possibility as a critical and oppositional medium, and is so to the extent that 'contemporary art cannot escape the accusation of passivity, uselessness even' (Virilio 2003b: 93). This assertion forms the crux of Virilio's polemic against contemporary art. In its most basic terms this polemic asserts that the scene of contemporary art is narrow and secretly authoritarian in its attitude to the potential diversity of artistic techniques and that it is unable to engage with the world, to understand, criticize or oppose emergent realities of collective political and social experience.

To this extent Virilio sees contemporary art being, by default, deeply complicit with the media culture of late industrial capitalism and with the concentration of power and wealth in the hands of a capital-holding elite. On this he is, at various points, very direct:

> from VIDEO ART onwards, no one can hear talk of CONCEPT ART without hearing the background noise of the mass media concealed behind the words and things of the art market.
>
> (Virilio 2003b: 77–8)

> It is certain that what has been called the inflation of the art market is
> a delirium more in relation with the multinationals than with artistic
> expression.
>
> (Virilio and Baj 2003: 15)

As far as Virilio is concerned the art market is nothing other than a vast
enterprise of commodification or commoditization by which the objects of
art are reduced to the status of exchangeable goods which serve to recycle
the vast quantities of excess wealth generated by electronic flows of capital
that govern contemporary global markets. Exemplary in this respect would
be the role played by Charles Saatchi in the development of the global art
market in the closing decades of the last century. Virilio is rather scathing
in his reference to Saatchi, pointing to a situation in which 'An advertiser
can transform anyone into an artist who will be able to sell a photo for
millions' (Virilio and Baj 2003: 15). He also cites figures such as Jeff Koons
and Damien Hirst as examples of people whom Saatchi has promoted
but who have no technical artistic talent *per se* (since they tend to work
with ready-mades or collective workshop constructions) (Virilio and Baj
2003: 16). This environment has led to what Virilio characterizes as an
'official art', that is, an art whose parameters are policed by a relatively small
quantity of museum directors and private sponsors such as Saatchi, and
whose existence is financially underpinned by an art market which is deeply
rooted in the mechanisms of contemporary media culture and global capital.
It is this situation which shapes and sustains the silence of contemporary art
and which removes from art its capacity to challenge and oppose. The
potential of art, which, for Virilio, 'has always been maintained in its life
through debate between opponents and partisans', is suppressed by 'an
official art around which a procedure of consensus, obedience and silence
is established' (Virilio and Baj 2003: 14). Whether we like it or not, as
Virilio would say, art has become passive, complicit, and useless.

THE ACCIDENT OF ART

As was indicated earlier Virilio's discourse on the recent historical
development and current state of the visual and plastic arts is polemical
and outspoken and likely to be disputed by many as too negative or one-
sided. One could object, for instance, that the range of techniques within
contemporary art is not as narrow or restrictive as he claims. For example,
the prominence, at the time of writing this study, of Chris Offili's work

suggests that painting has not been entirely erased from the canon of acceptable forms in the way that Virilio sometimes suggests. One could also object that his highly critical understanding of what he calls 'motorized art' betrays a barely concealed attitude of technophobia which prevents Virilio from engaging fully with the way in which the art of recent decades has explored the implications of technology, its impact on experience, perception and what it means to be human (all eminently Virilian concerns).

It is worth noting once again, however, that Virilio has always denied being technophobic or indeed pessimistic in his account of technology and its impact within the cultural and political space of twentieth and twenty-first-century modernity. In his interview with Enrico Baj he insists, rather, that:

> I am not at all pessimistic. I am seeking to be realistic and to understand the way in which the twentieth century has been a pitiless century, as Albert Camus said, the century of the *Titanic*, of Chernobyl, of Auschwitz and of Hiroshima. One mustn't be pessimistic but realistic.
>
> (Virilio and Baj 2003: 36–7)

In the late 1990s and early 2000s Virilio has developed a theory of the 'accident' in order to articulate more fully his critical response to technology and technological innovation. He may have done so to counter accusations that his outlook and analysis are characterized by excessive pessimism or technophobia. Interestingly, his theory of the accident such as it has been developed in recent years is closely linked to his understanding of art. Indeed, his increasing interest in art at the beginning of this current decade accompanies his more or less sustained exposition of the theory of the accident.

Virilio has described himself variously as an 'art critic of technology' (Armitage 2001: 25) or as a 'critic of the technical arts' (Virilio and Baj 2003: 51). Such comments reflect the way in which his dromological discourse on technology and the techno-scientific world view is not itself technical, sociological or that of a political scientist. Rather, as was suggested in the very first chapter, his perspective is rooted in the question of perspective itself, in a critical approach to fundamental ways of seeing or perceiving the world. To this extent it perhaps has more in common with art than it does with science. In an interview with John Armitage Virilio suggests that 'I am not fretting against technology *per se* but against the logic behind it' (Armitage 2001: 25). Fundamental to that hidden logic of technology, he contends, are the existence and necessary occurrence of accidents. In his interview with Enrico Baj Virilio sums up his theory of the accident in very straightforward and accessible terms: 'There is no technical invention without accidents. Each time a technology is invented, a technology of transport, of transmission, or of information, a specific accident is born' (Virilio and Baj 2003: 29). In *The Original Accident* he develops this idea further: 'a shipwreck is the . . . invention of the ship, the air crash that of the supersonic plane, just as Chernobyl is the invention of the nuclear power station' (Virilio 2005c: 18). Elsewhere in the same work he adds: 'To invent the train is to invent the accident of derailment. To invent the domestic car is to produce the pile-up on the motorway' (Virilio 2005c: 27). What Virilio is suggesting with this theory of the accident is that technological progress can never be cast in simply or straightforwardly positive terms. The traditional ideology of progress would tell us that the history of technical development obeys an inevitable logic of incremental improvement. According to this logic humans develop ever more efficient tools for controlling the natural world and for meeting specifically human goals and aspirations (e.g. greater material wealth, or better health and longevity). Such an ideology is, Virilio suggests, unrealistic or, more specifically, unsustainable in the face of the often catastrophic events that have accompanied technical development in the twentieth century. In his approach to technology he is not aiming simply to subvert this ideology of progress by inverting its terms so that all technical development would be seen as negative rather than positive. Virilio's claim is, rather, that our tendency to see innovation in entirely positive terms blinds us to its negative aspects. His theory of the accident, and his work more generally, represent an attempt to 'discover the hidden truth of our successes', to offer what he calls an 'ACCIDENTAL REVELATION' but one which would be 'in no way apocalyptic' (Virilio 2005c: 28). With technological successes comes the inevitability of technological failures or accidents and this leads Virilio to affirm 'the henceforth unavoidable necessity of EXPOSING THE ACCIDENT' (Virilio 2005c: 28).

Virilio's aim, then, in his theory of the accident, as elsewhere in his work, is not to be negative or pessimistic but rather to uncover the hidden negativity within phenomena that we tend to collectively judge in positive terms. The difference between being negative and revealing hidden negativity may appear rather small to some but for Virilio it is absolutely decisive. In so far as the aim of his work is to reveal, to expose, or to challenge received ways of seeing the world, it obeys a logic which is similar to that which he ascribes to art and the artwork. Although his writing is preoccupied with questions of technology, of techno-science, and the culture of acceleration which modern technology has brought about, Virilio takes care to differentiate between art and science and to align his own work with the latter rather than the former. It is in this context that he comes to speak of 'the accident of art' and that the theory of the accident and his discourse on art more generally come together:

> Above all, art is not a science or a technoscience. Art and science are two different things. But is there an accident of art? Yes, the accident of art is representation. It is that one comes to view the world differently. . . . Artists are creators of reality by means of a new vision of the world. The accident in this case is constituted by one vision which comes to replace another. Art is what renews our vision of the world.
>
> (Virilio and Baj 2003: 30–1)

This notion of the accident of art rearticulates Virilio's belief that art is a medium of expression which is critical and oppositional. The critical and oppositional gesture of art is, however, not simply the destruction, contestation or negation of existing forms. Nor does this gesture tie art to the expression of any specific or programmatic oppositional politics or ideology. Rather this oppositional gesture carries with it a positive force of creation and renewal. What necessarily break up, fail or are undone by the techniques of artistic expression are received ways of thinking and seeing. The critical or 'accidental' function of art is, for Virilio, one in which the techniques of artistic expression (e.g. painterly and sculptural techniques, or the techniques of writing) combine to show or reveal the world in a new and different way. There is no art without criticism and no criticism without art, or as Virilio himself puts it: 'You cannot be an artist if you are not at the same time a critic, if you do not know how to be critical of what you do. Me, across all my works, I am a critic of the technical arts' (Virilio and Baj 2003: 51).

It would seem, then, that Virilio's discourse on modern art, on its silence, and on the 'accident of art' brings this discussion back to the point where it began in the opening chapters. There it was argued that his writing needed to be understood in relation to insights he derived from his early work as a painter and that, rather than being negative or pessimistic, his critical perspectives develop from an attempt to engage with the politics of perception. Across the three decades or so, during which time Virilio has published over twenty full-length works and an even greater number of articles, his writing has sought to respond with a sense of urgency to the challenge posed to our understanding by technological change in the twentieth century and now the early twenty-first. His writing is polemical, provocative and develops its ideas in what can sometimes appear to be a rather haphazard or provisional manner. It should be evident from the discussion of the preceding chapters, however, that this apparently haphazard manner is informed by an underlying continuity of critical thinking and a consistency of theoretical or 'dromological' approach. In aligning his discourse with the perspective of art, Virilio eschews the systematic method of sociological analysis or political science. Yet he does so in order to perform a critical work which operates on a fundamental philosophical and conceptual level. In *The Original Accident* he asserts that 'the urgency of an "intelligence of the crisis of intelligence" has shown itself at the beginning of the twenty-first century' (Virilio 2005c: 19). We need to come to terms, he suggests, with the limitations of our technical inventiveness and to thoroughly rethink our confidence in the limitlessness of human progress and technological innovation. What we need is nothing less than 'a philosophy of post-industrial ESCHATOLOGY' (Virilio 2005c: 19). Our inherited belief systems concerning the destiny of humanity, what Virilio here calls eschatology, are, he contends, insufficient when it comes to understanding what may be at stake in our technological present or future. If we blithely assume that the destiny of the human is ever increasing technological progress or technical dominance over the space of the earth and its resources, then we will never understand or come to terms with the underlying negativity which has expressed itself in so many disasters over the past hundred years: the two World Wars, Auschwitz, Hiroshima and Nagasaki, Chernobyl and countless other events whose catastrophic proportions have been determined by the power of technological innovation. This, at least, is the warning Virilio gives us as an art critic of technology. The accident of art, its power to renew our vision of the world, works in his writing as a whole as a means of understanding and philosophically responding to the necessity and inevitability of the technological accident.

SUMMARY

Virilio sees the creativity of art as rooted in the embodied sensory and worldly experience of the artist. Consequently he believes that art as an expressive medium should be engaged with the representation of worldly reality and that art has a critical and oppositional function. It should challenge our received ways of viewing the world and renew our vision of it. The account Virilio offers of modern and contemporary art is itself critical and oppositional. He relates the dissolution of form within twentieth-century art and its tendency to move towards ever greater degrees of abstraction to the impact of the two World Wars on individual and collective artistic experience. He also sees a diminishing of the representational function of art as resulting from the tendency of modern visual media (cinema, video, digital photography) to diminish the spatial realm of material existence in favour of the temporal realm of exposure or presentation of an image. Modern art and contemporary art emerge in this context as forms which are essentially passive, divorced from the realities and politics of the real world. Against this backdrop Virilio affirms the 'accident of art', that is, the way in which artistic representation overturns received ways of seeing the world to create new and different forms of vision. For Virilio the accident of art can allow us to respond differently to the ideology of technology and to understand the way in which the hidden negativity of technical invention means that technological accidents are necessary and inevitable.

AFTER VIRILIO

Given the broad scope of Virilio's writing it is hardly surprising that his work has been influential in a number of areas. He has made an impact in the field of war and international relations theory. He has exerted an increasingly significant influence in the areas of media and social theory and his thought has also informed some recent developments in thinking about urbanism and the politics of ecology. The publication of his interview with Sylvère Lotringer, *Pure War*, perhaps did most to introduce Virilio's writing to an English-speaking readership and, in consequence, it was arguably in the areas of war theory and international politics that his presence was first felt in the anglophone world. In a short piece dating from 1986 which appears in a collected volume of essays entitled *International/Intertextual Relations*, Michael Shapiro cites *Pure War* (Virilio and Lotringer 1997) in order to analyse what he calls: 'The modern text of international danger' (Der Derian and Shapiro 1986: 20). Pure war, it will be remembered, can be understood both as a military strategy based on generalized insecurity (nuclear deterrence) and as a figure for a global techno-scientific organization of states. According to Shapiro's account, pure war, as elaborated by Virilio, offers a key conceptual tool for understanding the 'demise of a political perspective on the production of international danger' (Der Derian and Shapiro 1986: 20). The techno-scientific world view embodied in the logic of pure war is put forward as an underlying cause of the contemporary death of politics.

This tendency to use Virilio's writing to articulate new ways of thinking about war, international security and international relations has been developed further by James Der Derian (Der Derian 1992, 2001). In his influential 1992 work, *Antidiplomacy*, Der Derian argues that Virilio has 'almost single-handedly brought the issue of speed back into social and political theory' (Der Derian 1992: 130). The Lotringer interview *Pure War* is once again cited and the concept itself plays a key role in Der Derian's analysis. He suggests, for instance, that 'terrorism has emerged as [pure war's] most virulent expression' (Der Derian 1992: 115). He also argues that reading Virilio will allow a deeper understanding of the manner in which the strategic field of security and international relations has been transformed and identifies, in particular, the displacement of space by time as a key element in this transformation. In a slightly later essay Der Derian offers a reinterpretation of realist theory in international relations. Realism as a theory of international relations was originally elaborated in 1948 by Hans Morganthau in *Politics Among Nations* (Morgenthau 1993) and developed into its 'neo-realist' form by Kenneth Waltz in his 1979 work, *Theory of International Politics* (Waltz 1979). Broadly speaking the realist approach to international politics views relations between states as a function of competing interests defined in terms of power. It also stresses the notion of rational order within the study of politics. Referring to Virilio, Der Derian affirms that 'a dromology of realism is required'. He also once again suggests also that 'the ascendancy of temporality over spatiality in world politics' requires us to rethink some of the basic tenets of international relations theory (Der Derian 1995: 369). Dromology, he argues, can, along with other important concepts drawn from the area of contemporary French thought, provide the international relations theorist with 'new deconstructive tools *and* antidiplomatic strategies to reinterpret realism' (Der Derian 1995: 369–70). Der Derian is not the only theorist to draw on Virilio in order to analyse questions of contemporary security and international politics. In their co-authored work *The Postmodern Adventure*, Stephen Best and Douglas Kellner draw on Virilio's analyses in order to develop an understanding of postmodern warfare. In particular they read Virilio in order to 'elucidate the postmodern features of the Persian Gulf TV war' (Best and Kellner 2001: 73). Their analysis centres around his critique of the accelerated speeds of modern technologies and the increased pace of destruction afforded by contemporary military weapons systems. In so far as Virilio sees the modern war machine as the 'demiurge of technological growth' Best and Kellner argue that Virilio allows us to think the negative potential of technical innovation (Best and Kellner 2001: 89).

In the field of media and social theory Virilio's work has been used to understand the transformation of modern culture which has been brought about by technological developments such as photography, cinema and digital media. In *Visions of Modernity* (1998) Scott McQuire offers an extended theoretical and historical account of the impact of photography on modes of perception, cognition and systems of knowledge from the late nineteenth century onwards. Although he draws on a wide range of theoretical sources, Virilio's concept of a 'logistics of perception' is of decisive importance for McQuire's work and, in particular, informs his analysis of the transformation of perceptual modes brought about by cinema in the early twentieth century. McQuire argues that cinema 'does not merely produce other perceptions, but the *other* of embodied perception' (McQuire 1998: 80). This clearly recalls Virilio's 'aesthetics of disappearance' and his account of telepresence. Following Virilio closely, McQuire suggests that the cine-spectator 'is free to roam many worlds, unmoored in time and space . . . but is perhaps at risk of losing all homes, as the here and now is set adrift in the infinite migrations of the nowhere' (McQuire 1998: 91). McQuire's account of television and of 'television's perceptual logistics' also follows Virilio. The 'televisual present' is a time which privileges instantaneity over the historical time of duration, fosters collective amnesia and suppresses considered reflection and judgement (McQuire 1998: 129–30). Virilio's account of the virtualization of experience brought about by modern broadcast media is also taken up in the work of the social theorist Sean Cubitt. In his 1998 work *Digital Aesthetics* Cubitt cites Virilio and argues that the 'infinity of the virtual' has taken the place of the divine within contemporary life and that this has brought with it a radical alteration in our collective experience of time according to which 'the external expansion of the future' is turned into 'the internal dematerialized expansion of the present' (Cubitt 1998: 84). Virilio occupies a much larger place in Cubitt's 2001 work *Simulation and Social Theory*. Here he argues that Virilio allows us to understand the way in which the electronic mediation of vision in modern social forms has led to 'the abolition of the weight, mass, bulk and depth of truth' and an 'implosion of the human' (Cubitt 2001: 61, 64). Virilio's thinking not only allows us to understand the virtualization of experience brought about by modern media, Cubitt suggests, it also offers insight into the impact of virtualization on subjectivity (Cubitt 2001: 79).

If Virilio's account of the becoming virtual of modern life describes the wasting of spatial experience in favour of an increasingly dominant temporal dimension, it is not surprising that it should be of interest to urbanists and environmental thinkers. In a collection of essays entitled *The Hieroglyphs of Space* (Leach 2002), Sarah Chaplin and Eric Holding suggest that Virilio's concerns 'strike at the heart of a new visual and spatial analysis of the city' (Leach 2002: 187). Virilio, they argue, can offer theoretical perspectives in order to elaborate a critical understanding of what might be called an experience of the 'post-urban'. In *The Environment in Poststructuralist Thought* Verena Andermatt Conley appeals to Virilio in order to understand the way in which contemporary life occurs 'in the aftermath of the collapse of measured time and space' (Conley 1997: 84). She relates this to possibilities of thinking about environmental or ecological politics. The notion of ecological struggle, Conley points out, has always been a central preoccupation of Virilio's work (Conley 1997: 80). In allowing us to think critically about the transformation of spatial experience and modes of subjectivity, Virilio's writing may help us to articulate specific demands in the area of ecological and environmental politics. In particular Conley suggests that Virilio can help us to ground the demand for 'a re-establishment of *memory* built on topical spaces, real experience and shared discourses' (Conley 1997: 87).

Despite this broad range of disciplines in which Virilio's work has been taken up, there remain areas in which his thought is likely to make an important contribution but has yet to make a significant impact. These might include art criticism and film studies (Virilio, for instance, made an important contribution to a volume on the work of the Canadian film maker Atom Egoyan (Desbarats *et al.* 1993)). Above all Virilio's thinking will no doubt continue to offer rich resources for future contributions in the philosophy of technology. Although his positions are clearly tied to the phenomenological thought of Husserl and Merleau-Ponty, they would be of interest still to a critical-philosophical thought that has moved beyond phenomenology and its key concept of phenomenological presence. This is borne out in the work undertaken by the French philosopher Bernard Stiegler on technics and time in the 1990s and early 2000s (Stiegler 1994, 1996, 2001). Steigler's *Technics* and *Time* trilogy (set to become a cycle of five books) is arguably a major event in contemporary French philosophy. It draws on the work of important twentieth-century figures such as that archaeologist and anthropologist André Leroi-Gourhan (1911–1986) and thinkers of technology such as Gilbert Simondon (1926–87). It also offers a broadly Derridean deconstructive account of Husserlian and Heiddeggarian thinking about technology in relation to questions of temporality. In this respect Stiegler's work moves firmly beyond the classical phenomenological perspective in so far as it suggests that human experience is thoroughly permeated by technical life at its very origin. Virilio is nevertheless a key influence for Stiegler, who argues that contemporary culture is undergoing a process of industrialization of memory which alters the manner in which experience and events unfold. He relates this to the proliferation of modes of direct communication which are able to transmit data in real time and work to diminish cultural processes which were previously underpinned by techniques of writing (see for instance Stiegler 1996: 17).

The opening chapter of this study drew attention to Arthur Kroker's work *The Possessed Individual* and cited his comment that 'Contemporary French thought consists of a creative, dynamic and highly original account of technological society' (Kroker 1992: 2). Stiegler's philosophical work on technics has shown even more clearly the extent to which the question of technology thoroughly permeates key aspects of modern French thought. The influence of dromology on thinkers such as Stiegler highlights further Virilio's importance within the wider terrain of recent and contemporary French philosophy. It also shows that the interest of Virilio's writing is in no way limited by his residual attachment to notions of phenomenological presence and his mourning or nostalgia for a lost immediacy of perceptual experience. Such an immediacy of experience may indeed be subject to a process of erosion by the technologies which so thoroughly permeate culture in post-industrial society. Whether this is an inherently negative phenomenon cannot be decided here and will, necessarily, remain the subject of critical and philosophical debate.

The key point is that Virilio's writing opens up a perspective on the nature of technological modernity which is entirely different from the technocratic discourses which circulate prominently within public debate. It has been argued from the beginning of this study that Virilio's works are provocative and polemical. They aim to disrupt our received discourses and habitual ways of seeing the world. Rooted in a fundamental concern with the politics of perception, Virilio's writing takes technology as its key theme in order to question the broader horizons of our collective experience and the manner in which they are structured and organized. To this extent it is clear that Virilio will remain an indispensable point of reference for future critical and philosophical debates regarding the nature of technology and its impact upon human perception and experience.

Above all Virilio's work allows us to address fundamental questions about the nature of our shared history, about contemporary culture, and about the future directions post-industrial society may take. If we want to ask fundamental questions about what has happened to human society during the last century and, in particular, during the last few decades, then the concepts of dromology, virtualization, telepresence and pure war will allow us to think critically in ways which were not possible before Virilio. Technological change has arguably occurred at rate which outstrips the ability of traditional concepts to account for that change. If this is so, then new concepts which allow us to account for such rapid change are of fundamental importance. In the same way, social and political transformation may also be occurring at a rate which potentially outstrips the ability of our existing forms of knowledge to understand what is at stake. Again, the innovative critical thinking developed by Virilio can be seen as an indispensable means of understanding the contemporary world and its future development.

Indeed, Virilio's work is as much orientated toward the future as it is toward the past and the present. It offers rich resources for any attempt to think about 'post-industrial eschatology'. It suggests ways of fundamentally rethinking what the destiny of humanity might be. The ends of technology and the goals of technological society have, after Virilio, been provocatively and urgently called into question.

FURTHER READING

Nearly all of Virilio's full-length works have been translated into English. The surprising exception to this is his second major publication, *L'Insécurité du territoire*, which initially appeared in 1976. Some of his most recent works have also yet to appear in English at the time of writing this study. Only these untranslated texts have been listed in their original French editions. All other references are to the English editions. Throughout this study all the cited translations of Virilio into English have been modified.

The best work for those coming to Virilio for the first time is *Negative Horizon*, which was published in the original French in 1984. This work covers all of his major concerns relating to perception, the construction of space, dromology, media and war. Those interested primarily in Virilio's account of perception, modern media and the becoming virtual of experience should then read *Lost Dimension*, *Polar Inertia* and *The Vision Machine*. Those more interested in the account he gives of war and politics should tackle early works such as *Bunker Archeology*, *Speed and Politics* or *Popular Defense and Ecological Struggles* and then proceed to later work such as *Desert Screen* and *Strategy of Deception*. Anyone wishing to pursue Virilio's account of modern electronic and digital media further should read *The Information Bomb* and *Open Sky*. Because Virilio writes in an open-ended, often fragmentary manner, and because his insights and arguments are formed through a process of accumulation, readers are advised to cover a number of works in order to engage with his writing and avoid relying on any one text. For a more comprehensive bibliography of Virilio's books and essays in French and English see Armitage (2001: 202–11).

WORKS BY PAUL VIRILIO

Virilio, P. (1986) *Speed and Politics*, trans. M. Polizzotti, New York: Semiotext(e). Published originally in 1977, Virilio's first work examining the impact of speed on politics throughout history is a key point of departure for his later work.

Virilio, P. (1989) *War and Cinema*, trans. P. Camiller, London: Verso. Examines the interrelation of photographic and cinematic technology on the waging of war from the First World War onwards.

Virilio, P. (1990) *Popular Defense and Ecological Struggles*, trans. M. Polizzotti, New York: Semiotext(e). Here Virilio deals with the origins of warfare and of military space and also examines the way in which social space and political struggle are shaped by vectors of speed and modes of transport.

Virilio, P. (1991a) *The Lost Dimension*, trans. D. Moshenberg, New York: Semiotext(e). Published originally in 1984 as *L'Espace critique*, this is Virilio's major work on the transformation of space brought about by modern transport and communications.

Virilio, P. (1991b) *The Aesthetics of Disappearance*, trans. P. Beitchman, New York: Semiotext(e). Dating from 1980, this work is the first to introduce this key notion in Virilio's thinking. In particular it gives an account of the transformation of perceptual modes brought about by cinema.

Virilio, P. (1993) *L'Insécurité du territoire*, second edition, Paris: Galilée. This work extends Virilio's analysis of *Bunker Archeology* and develops key political concepts such as 'total peace'.

Virilio, P. (1994a) *Bunker Archeology*, trans. G. Collins, New York: Princeton Architectural Press. Virilio incorporates his own photographs of the Atlantic Second World War bunkers in this founding analysis of the relation between military and political space.

Virilio, P. (1994b) *The Vision Machine*, trans. J. Rose, London: British Film Institute. This is an extended account of the impact of modern visual media on individual perception and collective experience.

Virilio, P. (1995) *The Art of the Motor*, trans. J. Rose, Minneapolis MN: University of Minnesota Press. Virilio gives an account of the impact of modern visual media on perception and aesthetic forms.

Virilio, P. (1997a) *Open Sky*, trans. J. Rose, London: Verso. Virilio continues his account of the modern media, their impact on the organization of space and the becoming virtual of experience.

Virilio, P. (2000a) *The Information Bomb*, trans. C. Turner, London: Verso. In this work Virilio extends his account of the impact of digital media and communication on social forms.

Virilio, P. (2000b) *A Landscape of Events*, trans. J. Rose, Cambridge MA: MIT Press. In this work Virilio argues that modern technology has changed the way in which events occur and historical temporality unfolds.

Virilio, P. (2000c) *Strategy of Deception*, trans. C. Turner, London: Verso. Virilio extends the account of contemporary warfare developed initially in *Desert Screen*.

Virilio, P. (2000d) *Polar Inertia*, trans. P. Camiller, London: Sage. This is the key work in which Virilio introduces concepts such as light-time and in which he suggests that modern technologies of speed and electronic viewing risk reducing us to a state of immobility and incarceration.

Virilio, P. (2002) *Ground Zero*, trans. C. Turner, London: Verso. In this work Virilio extends his account of chronopolitcs, contemporary warfare and technocratic culture and social organization.

Virilio, P. (2003a) *Unknown Quantity*, London: Thames and Hudson. This is a catalogue which accompanied an exhibition by Virilio held at the Fondation Cartier in Paris in which his theory of the accident is developed.

Virilio, P. (2003b) *Art and Fear*, trans. J. Rose, London: Continuum. In this work Virilio offers an extended polemic against the state of contemporary art.

Virilio, P. (2005a) *Negative Horizon*, trans. M. Degener, London: Continuum. A major work by Virilio which, develops all the major themes and concerns of his thinking.

Virilio, P. (2005b) *City of Panic*, trans. J. Rose, Oxford: Berg. Virilio continues his critique of modern warfare and 'infowar'; he also develops further his thinking about global strategic space and the impact of speed on the ecology of space.

Virilio, P. (2005c) *L'Accident originel*, Paris: Galilée. Here Virilio develops further his theory of the accident.

Virilio, P. (2005d) *L'Art à perte de vue*, Paris. Galilée. In this volume Virilio continues his meditation on contemporary art.

Virilio, P. (2005e) *Desert Screen: War at the Speed of Light*, trans. M. Degener, London: Continuum. This is Virilio's groundbreaking critique of the first Gulf war, taken by many to be a critical analysis of postmodern warfare.

Virilio, P. and Parent, C. (1996) *Architecture Principe 1966 et 1996*, Paris: Éditions de l'imprimeur. This volume collects all the issues of this key avant-garde architectural journal of the 1960s, on which Virilio collaborated with Claude Parent. It also includes material giving a retrospective perspective on the work of the review.

Virilio, P. and Parent, C. (1999) *The Function of the Oblique: The Architecture of Claude Parent and Paul Virilio 1963–1969*, trans. P. Johnston, London: Architectural Association. This is an account of the theoretical perspective developed by Virilio in his collaboration with Parent.

INTERVIEWS WITH PAUL VIRILIO

Virilio is a highly prolific giver of interviews. Listed below are the those interviews he has given which have been gathered into full-length volumes. For a full bibliographical list of Virilio's interviews in French and English see Armitage's *Virilio Live* listed below (Armitage 2001: 205–6, 209–11).

Armitage, J. (2001) *Virilio Live: Selected Interviews*, London: Sage. A collection of interviews with a number of different interlocutors.

Virilio, P. (1997b) *Voyage d'hiver*, Marseille: Éditions Paranthèses. A series of interviews with Marianne Brausch touching on questions of urbanism and architecture.

Virilio, P. (1999) *The Politics of the Very Worst*, trans. M. Cavaliere and S. Lotringer, New York: Semiotext(e). Virilio discusses technology and politics with Philippe Petit.

Virilio, P. and Baj, E. (2003) *Discours sur l'horreur de l'art*, Lyon: Atelier de création libertaire. Virilio discusses art with the Italian anarchist and avant-garde artist, Enrico Baj.

Virilio, P. and Lotringer, S. (1997) *Pure War*, trans. B. O'Keefe, second edition, New York: Semiotext(e). Virilio develops this key concept in discussion with Sylvère Lotringer.

Virilio, P. and Lotringer, S. (2002) *Crepuscular Dawn*, trans. M. Taormina, New York: Semiotext(e). Virilio develops his thinking about biotechnology in his discussion with Lotringer.

Virilio, P. and Lotringer, S. (2005) *The Accident of Art*, London: Semiotext(e). Virilio continues his discourse on modern art and the question of the accident in these interviews.

WORKS ON VIRILIO

Listed below are those full-length works dedicated to Virilio and the two existing Virilio readers. Those works which deal partly with Virilio have been mentioned in the chapter 'After Virilio' and are listed under works cited.

Armitage, J., ed. (2000) *Paul Virilio: From Modernism to Hypermodernism and Beyond*, London: Sage. A valuable collection of critical essays on Virilio covering all the major aspects of his work.

Der Derian, J. ed. (1998) *The Virilio Reader*, Oxford: Blackwell. An excellent collection of introductory readings of Virilio.

Redhead, S. (2004a) *Paul Virilio: Theorist for an Accelerated Culture*, Edinburgh: Edinburgh University Press. The first single-author, full-length work to be published on Virilio in English.

Redhead, S. (2004b) *The Paul Virilio Reader*, Edinburgh: Edinburgh University Press. The second volume of introductory readings on Virilio to be published in English.

WORKS CITED

Apollonio, U. (1973) *Futurist Manifestos*, trans. R. Brain *et al.*, Boston MA: MFA Publications.

Baudrillard, J. (1995) *The Gulf War did not Take Place*, trans. P. Patton, Sydney: Power Publications.

Benjamin, W. (1974) *Illuminations*, trans. H. Zohn, London: Fontana.

Best, S. and Kellner, D. (2001) *The Postmodern Adventure: Science, Technology, and Cultural Studies at the Third Millennium*, London: Routledge.

Clausewitz, C. (1968) *On War*, trans. J. J. Graham, Harmondsworth: Penguin.

Conley, V. A. (1997) *The Environment in Poststructuralist Thought*, London: Routledge.

Crosby, A. (1997) *The Measure of Reality*, Cambridge: Cambridge University Press.

Cubitt, S. (1998) *Digital Aesthetics*, London: Sage.

Cubitt, S. (2001) *Simulation and Social Theory*, London: Sage.

Davis, C. (2004) *After Poststructuralism: Reading, Stories, and Theory*, London: Routledge.

Deleuze, G. (2001) *Difference and Repetition*, trans. P. Patton, London: Continuum.

Der Derian, J. (1992) *Antidiplomacy: Spies, Terror, Speed, and War*, Oxford: Blackwell.

Der Derian, J. (ed.) (1995) *International Theory: Critical Investigations*, Basingstoke: Macmillan.

Der Derian, J. (2001) *Virtuous War: Mapping the Military–Industrial–Media– Entertainment Network*, Boulder CO: Westview Press.

Der Derian, J. and Shapiro, M. J. (1986) *International/Intertextual Relations*, Lexington MA: Lexington Books.

Derrida, J. (1997) *Of Grammatology*, trans. G. C. Spivak, Baltimore MD: Johns Hopkins University Press.

Derrida, J. (2005) *On Touching – Jean-Luc Nancy*, trans. C. Irizarry. Stanford CA: Stanford University Press.

Desbarats, C., Lageira, J. *et al.* (1993) *Atom Egoyan*, Paris: Dis Voir.

Descartes, R. (1999) *Discourse on Method*, trans. D. Clark, London: Penguin.

Ellul, J. (1965) *The Technological Society*, trans. J. Wilkinson, London: Jonathan Cape.

Foucault, M. (1995) *Discipline and Punish*, trans. A. Sheridan, London: Vintage.

Heidegger, M. (1962) *Being and Time*, trans. J. MacQuarrie, Oxford: Blackwell.

Heidegger, M. (1993) *Basic Writings*, ed. D. Farrell Krell, London: Routledge.

Husserl, E. (1970) *The Crisis of European Sciences and Transcendental Phenomenology*, trans. D. Carr, Evanston IL: Nothwestern University Press.

Husserl, E. (1997) *Thing and Space. 1907 Lectures, Collected Works* VII, trans. R. Rojcewicz, Dordrecht: Kluwer.

James, I. (2006) 'Phenomenology in Diaspaora: Paul Virilio and the Question of Technology' in *French Cultural Studies*, 17 (3), London: Sage.

Joly, C. (2004) *Claude Parent, Paul Virilio, Église Sainte-Bernadette à Nevers*, Paris: J.-M. Place.

Kaplan, D. M. (2004) *Readings in the Philosophy of Technology*, Lanham MD: Rowman and Littlefield.

Kroker, A. (1992) *The Possessed Individual: Technology and the French Postmodern*, New York: St Martin's Press.

Leach, N. (ed.) (2002) *The Hieroglyphs of Space: Reading and Experiencing the Modern Metropolis*, London: Routledge.

Leslie, E. (2000) *Walter Benjamin: Overpowering Conformism*, London: Pluto.

Martin, L. H. (1998) *Technologies of the Self*, Amherst MA: University of Massachusetts Press.

McQuire, S. (1998) *Visions of Modernity: Representation, Memory, Time and Space in the Age of the Camera*, London: Sage.

Merleau-Ponty, M. (2002) *Phenomenology of Perception*, trans. C. Smith. London: Routledge.

Morgenthau, H. (1993) *Politics Among Nations*, New York: McGraw-Hill.

Plotnitsky, A. (2002) *The Knowable and the Unknowable: Modern Science, Nonclassical thought and the 'Two Cultures'*, Ann Arbor MI: University of Michigan Press.

Smith, A. (1993) *The Wealth of Nations*, Oxford: Oxford University Press.

Sokal, A. and Bricmont J. (1998) *Intellectual Impostures: Postmodern Philosophers' Abuse of Science*, London: Profile.

Stiegler, B. (1994) *Technics and Time* I, *The Fault of Epimetheus*, trans. R. Beardsworth and G. Collins, Stanford CA: Stanford University Press.

Stiegler, B. (1996) *La Technique et le temps* II, *La Désorientation*, Paris: Galilée.

Steigler, B (2001) *La Technique et le temps* III, *Le Temps du cinéma et la question du mal-être*, Paris: Galilée.

Sun Tzu (1963) *The Art of War*, Oxford: Oxford University Press.

Waltz, K. (1979) *Theory of International Relations*, Reading MA: Addison-Wesley.

Wilmotte, J.-M. (1999) *Architecture intérieure des villes*, Paris: Le Moniteur.

INDEX

Abbé Pierre 90
acceleration 4–5, 9, 17, 30
accident 116–18, 119
aesthetics of disappearance 49–53, 55, 58, 66, 82, 110
architecture 5, 10–12, 26
Armitage, J. 9, 30, 89–91, 115, 131
art 1, 107–19
associationism 20

Baj, E. 109–10, 115–16, 117
Baudelaire, C. 6
Benjamin, W. 5–6
Berlusconi, S. 101
Best, S. 122
Breton, A. 110
Bricmont, J. 36–7
bunkers 70–7, 80
Bush, G. W. 101

Chaplin, S. 124
cinema 3, 5, 50–3, 82–4, 87, 88, 108, 111, 119
Clausewitz, C. 40, 69, 77
Conley, V. A. 124
Crosby, A. 59

Cubitt, S. 123

Dadaism 109–10
Davis, C. 36
deceleration 4–5
democracy 101–3
Der Derian, J. 122, 131
Derrida, J. 8, 125
Descartes, R. 60
dromology 17, 29–31, 39–43, 45, 46, 53, 73, 87, 90, 104, 115, 122, 125–6; dromocracy 94; dromosphere 29, 31–7, 39, 40–1, 42; dromoscopy 29, 32–4, 43, 46

Einstein, A. 35–6, 39
Ellul, J. 10
embodiment 3, 9, 11–16, 24, 26, 31, 45, 47–8, 53, 65, 108, 110

forms 18–24
Foucault, M. 8
fourth front 81, 85–7, 88
future 65, 126

Galileo 6, 59

Gestalt psychology 10, 18–24, 26

Heidegger, M. 8, 13–14, 125; *Being and Time* 13
Holding, E. 124
Husserl, E. 5–7, 9, 12–14, 20, 21, 38, 124, 125; *The Crisis in European Sciences and Transcendental Phenomenology* 6, 59; natural attitude 15–17; *Thing and Space* 13, 38; transcendental ego 14

Joly, C. 10

Kant, E. 14
Kaplan, D. 4
Kellner, D. 91, 122
Kittler, F. 30
Koffka, K. 20
Köhler, W. 20
Kroker, A. 7, 125

Leroi-Gouhran, A. 124
Lotringer, S. 67, 77, 113, 121–2

Marinetti, F. W. 45
McQuire, S. 61, 123
Merleau-Ponty, M. 10, 13–15, 48, 59, 90, 124; body-subject 14; *Phenomenology of Perception* 13, 60
Morganthau, H. 122
Mounier, E. 90, 104
Murdoch, R. 101, 102

oblique function 11

painting 17–18
Parent, C. 10–11, 25, 26
perception 3, 5–7, 9–27, 31, 40, 47–8, 54, 65–6, 102, 123, 125; logistics of perception 81–5, 123; perceptual whole 19
personalism 90, 94, 103, 104
perspective 24
phenomenology 5–8, 10, 12–17, 26, 31, 34–7, 47, 65, 66; phenomenological method 7

Plotnitsky, A. 37
politics 25, 30, 63, 67–9, 73–4, 87, 89–105; chronopolitics 97–104, 105

Redhead, S. 80, 89, 131

Saatchi, C 114
Sartre, J.-P. 14
scientific knowledge 6–7, 24, 29, 34–7, 43
Shapiro, M. 121
Simondon, G. 124
Smith, A. 68
Sokal, A. 36–7
space 5, 7, 9, 11–12, 15–16, 24, 29, 38, 45, 47, 54–6, 65, 90; military space 68, 70–7, 82, 96; political space 68, 71, 86, 91–7, 104; speed-space 31–7, 39, 40, 42–3, 81
speed 4–5, 9, 15, 29–43, 46, 49, 55, 87, 90, 97; speed of light 34–7; speed machines 46–7, 56, 65
state 92–9, 104
Stiegler, B. 124–5
Sun Tzu 40, 72
surrealism 110

technology 3–8, 9, 12, 25, 26, 27, 30, 37, 46, 62–6, 78, 81, 91, 95, 100, 117, 119, 125
telecommunications 3–4, 30, 45, 46, 60, 66, 87, 91, 95, 97
telepresence 55, 58–66, 123, 126
television 3, 61–4, 82, 123
time 5, 11, 16, 36, 45, 47; light-time 37–9, 40, 42–3, 53, 54, 61; political time 97–104; real time 61–6, 87, 99–101, 104
total peace 77–81, 86, 88
transparency 56–9
transport 4, 30, 46, 91, 95–6

urbanism 5, 10–12, 26, 67–8, 88, 124; city space 90, 92–3, 96, 98–9

Virilio, P. passim; *The Accident of Art*, 107, 131; *The Aesthetics of Disappearance* 51, 107, 128; *Architecture principe* 10–12, 130; *Art and Fear* 108, 110, 112–14, 129; *L'Art à perte de vue* 107, 111, 130; *The Art of the Motor* 12, 107, 111, 129; *Bunker Archaeology* 70–8, 81, 88, 91, 95, 127, 128; *City of Panic* 46, 102, 129; *Desert Screen* 67, 84–6, 127; *Discours sur l'horreur de l'art* 107, 131; *The Function of the Oblique* 130; *Ground Zero* 129; *The Information Bomb* 36, 127, 129; *The Insecurity of Territory* 12, 45, 78, 91–2, 94–5, 100, 127, 128; *A Landscape of Events* 129; *The Lost Dimension* 12, 31, 47, 50, 53, 55, 127, 128; *Negative Horizon* 16–18, 29, 32, 41, 42, 46, 49, 93, 97, 107, 127, 129; *Open Sky* 32, 40–1, 96, 127, 129; *The Original Accident* 116, 118, 130; *Polar Inertia* 12, 32, 34–6, 38, 41, 42, 47, 55, 56, 127, 129; *Popular Defence and Ecological Struggles* 69–72, 79, 91, 127, 128; *Pure War* 121–2, 131; *Speed and Politics* 29, 68, 91, 93, 95, 127, 128; *The Strategy of Deception* 85, 127, 129; *Unknown Quantity* 129; *The Vision Machine* 12, 36, 47–8, 50, 55, 57, 59, 62, 64, 65, 102, 127, 128; *War and Cinema* 5, 82–4, 107, 128

virtualization 8, 43, 45–66, 87, 96–104, 123, 126; virtual presence 49, 52–3, 59–66, 82

vision machines 56–66

war 25, 26, 63, 67–88; First World War 69, 75, 82–4, 109; Gulf War 69; pure war 77–81, 88, 126; Second World War 72–8, 80, 84, 85, 87, 88, 109; Spanish Civil War 75; total war 76–8, 86

wave optics 53, 58, 66

Wertheimer, M. 20

Wilmotte, J.-M. 11

worker-priest movement, 89–90

Zurbrugg, N. 95

Related titles from Routledge

Remaking Media:
The struggle to democratize public communication
Robert A. Hackett and William K. Carroll

What is the political significance and potential of democratic media activism in the Western world today?

Remaking Media rides on a wave of political and scholarly attention to oppositional communication, triggered by the rise in the 1990s of the Zapatistas, internet activism, and IndyMedia. This attention has mostly focused on alternative media and the 'media strategies' of social movements – i.e., 'democratization through the media'. This book concerns democratization of the media themselves, efforts to transform the 'machinery of representation', as a distinctive field that is pivotal to other social struggles.

Remaking Media takes as its premise the existence of a massive 'democratic deficit' in the field of public communication. This deficit propels diverse struggles to reform and revitalize public communication in the North Atlantic heartland of globalization. It focuses on activism directed towards challenging and changing media content, practices, and structures, as well as state policies on media.

Hackett & Carroll's approach is innovative in its attention to an emerging social movement that appears at the cutting edge of cultural and political contention. The book is grounded in three scholarly traditions that provide interpretive resources for a study of democratic media activism: political theories of democracy, critical media scholarship, and the sociology of social movements. By synthesizing insights from these sources they provide a unique and timely reading of the contemporary struggle to democratize communication.

ISBN 13: 978-0-415-39468-0 (hbk)
ISBN 13: 978-0-415-39469-7 (pbk)

Available at all good bookshops
For ordering and further information please visit:
www.routledge.com

Related titles from Routledge

Media and Cultural Theory
Edited by James Curran and David Morley

Media & Cultural Theory brings together leading international scholars to address key issues and debates within media and cultural studies including:

- Media representations of the new woman in contemporary society
- The creation of self in lifestyle media
- The nature of cultural globalisation
- The rise of digital actors and media

These subjects are analysed through the use of contemporary media and film texts such as *Bridget Jones* and *The Lord of the Rings* trilogy as well as case studies of the US and UK after 9/11.

ISBN 13: 978-0-415-31704-7 (hbk)
ISBN 13: 978-0-415-31705-4 (pbk)

Available at all good bookshops
For ordering and further information please visit:
www.routledge.com

Related titles from Routledge

Media and Power
James Curran

Media and Power addresses three key questions about the relationship between media and society.

- How much power do the media have?
- Who really controls the media?
- What is the relationship between media and power in society?

In this major new book, James Curran reviews the different answers which have been given, before advancing original interpretations in a series of ground-breaking essays.

Media and Power also provides a guided tour of the major debates in media studies:

- What part did the media play in the making of modern society?
- How did 'new media' change society in the past?
- Will radical media research recover from its mid-life crisis?
- What are the limitations of the US-based model of 'communications' research?
- Is globalization disempowering national electorates or bringing into being a new, progressive global politics?
- Is public service television the dying product of the nation in an age of globalization?
- What can be learned from the 'third way' tradition of European media policy?

Curran's response to these questions provides both a clear introduction to media research and an innovative analysis of media power, written by one of the field's leading scholars.

ISBN13: 978-0-415-07739-2 (hbk)
ISBN13: 978-0-415-07740-8 (pbk)

Available at all good bookshops
For ordering and further information please visit:
www.routledge.com

Related titles from Routledge

Media/Theory: Thinking About Media and Communications

Shaun Moores

'A grasp of an enormous body of work is displayed adroitly . . . overall the book is a genuine contribution to the literature. It should help to shape the future of critical reflections on media institutions and practices.'
David Chaney, Emeritus Professor of Sociology, University of Durham

'This is an accomplished and elegant set of discussions, where an unusually broad range of theory from the humanities and social sciences, much of it to do with media but much of it not, is examined and organized.'
Graeme Turner, Professor of Cultural Studies, University of Queensland

Media/Theory is an accessible yet challenging guide to ways of thinking about media and communications in modern life.

Shaun Moores connects the analysis of media and communications with key themes in contemporary social theory:

- Time
- Space
- Relationships
- Meanings
- Experiences

He insists that media studies are not simply about studying media. Rather, they require an understanding of how technologically mediated communication is bound up with wider processes in the modern world, from the reproduction of social life on an everyday basis to the reorganisation of social relations on a global scale.

Drawing on ideas from a range of disciplines in the humanities and social sciences, *Media/Theory* makes a distinctive contribution towards rethinking the shape and direction of media studies today.

ISBN 13: 978-0-415-24383-4 (hbk)
ISBN 13: 978-0-415-24384-1 (pbk)
Available at all good bookshops
For ordering and further information please visit:
www.routledge.com